Keys to
Creative
Faith

Keys to Creative Faith

edited by
Walden Howard

WORD BOOKS, Publisher
Waco, Texas

Library of Congress catalog card number: 76–43136
ISBN #87680–815–1
Printed in the United States of America

Contents

Introduction

This book is designed to help you pick your way through an obstacle course that faces conscientious Christians.

If you're like me, you find yourself almost every day having to make choices that put you at odds with the prevailing sentiments of society. The choices often are not easy. If "the good old days" of the past seemed to be more certain and predictable, that surely isn't the case today. Sometimes an issue seems not only two-sided but many-sided, with equally sincere Christians coming at it from a variety of places, depending on their background, their understanding of biblical guidelines, and their particular perception of a situation.

What we may feel the need for is a chance to think through our values—but not only alone. We need the company of others who are asking the same questions, people with whom we can share our feelings and who can give us the kind of supportive feedback that can free us to make decisions clearly. And for that we may need some guidance.

This book is written to help meet that need. It is designed for use in small groups (study groups, church school classes, sharing groups), in workshops and weekend retreats, or wherever men and women want to engage in serious interaction on an experiential level. Eight issues are dealt with, beginning, in each case, with some background reading and followed by some experiential exercises. You may find a single exercise sufficient for a particular meeting. If so, there are several to choose from at the close of each chapter.

The articles and stories appeared first in FAITH/AT/ WORK as it focused on each of these themes. They came out of staff research, from talking the issues over with our readers, asking for their response to questionnaires and soliciting stories of their own struggles and learnings. As editor, I have personally participated in the search for answers and have found it an enormously stretching experience. I am a different person than I was when the process began. And I hope you will be too as you work your way thoughtfully through the material that follows.

The initial writing in each chapter is mine, followed in most cases by two or three stories or articles which "model" individual approaches to solutions. To listen as others struggle with an issue is more helpful than reading ready-made answers.

I am grateful to those who have thus made this book possible and for their granting permission to reprint their stories. And I am especially grateful to my associate, Al Hanner, Director of Leadership Development for Faith at Work, for providing the helpful experiential exercises.

WALDEN HOWARD

1.
SUCCESS

Success Is a Moving Target

SUCCESS is a moving target.

Just as you get it in your sights, growth and change come to you and your idea of success changes with you. Or you hit the bull's-eye for once, only to discover that "being successful" isn't what it was cracked up to be. Or you fail in some way and in the learning that follows, you get a clearer vision of what true success is.

What is success? Have you changed your idea of success in the past few years? Do you feel successful right now?

America, as a nation, is going through a time of fundamental change. Which is a way of saying that millions of men and women in America are questioning traditionally accepted norms and reaching for new values. Watergate and the energy crisis have contributed to the search, but the causes lie deeper than that.

In his monumental work, *The American Idea of Success* (McGraw-Hill, 1971), Richard M. Huber traces the fluctuating evolution of what most Americans have considered success. Hard work, thrift, obedience to God and kindness to one's neighbors—the Puritan ethic—Huber says, motivated most of the settlers who first came to these shores. They faced the arduous task of carving out a foothold on a strange continent. But as success came to them, as frontiers expanded, and the industrial revolution came of age, it became possible for people who had started with little to make a fortune. Enormous wealth began to come to a few individuals and the American myth of success was born.

It was the Horatio Alger era when any man worth his salt could rise from poverty to riches. If religious justification was needed, it was found in the belief that prosperity was a sign of God's blessing and in the fact that it enabled men to be great benefactors. P. T. Barnum declared, "Money getters are the benefactors of our race." Andrew Carnegie made millions of dollars but gave most of it away to public causes. Wealth which accrued, often at the expense of poverty and suffering among workers, was justified by the use to which it was put. But greed and selfishness were inherent in the scramble and are still a part of what we call the "American way of life."

The dream of "making it" is still the carrot on the stick that drives many Americans. But it is not simply how much money one can make that matters. It is where one starts and how far he goes in a lifetime. In a society that allows for upward mobility the measure is how far up one moves—in terms of prestige or power or influence as much as money. Money is simply a symbol—the symbol of what it can buy in power and prestige as well as comfort.

William H. Whyte, Jr., in his classic work, *The Organization Man* (Simon & Schuster, 1956), concludes, "The pursuit of individual salvation through hard work, thrift and competitive struggle is the heart of the American achievement." But, he adds, "by the time of the First World War, the Protestant Ethic had taken a shellacking from which it would not recover; rugged individualism and hard work had done wonders for the people to whom God in His infinite wisdom, as one put it, had given control of society. But it hadn't done well for everyone else."

Attention began to shift from the individual and his pursuit of success to the needs of the whole society. First through voluntary associations and increasingly through governmental action, relief has been offered to those who did not or could not "make it." And gradually we are beginning to measure success as a nation by the quality of life available to all our citizens, not simply to those who could win in the mad competitive scramble.

We are far from solving the inequities in our society, however. We pride ourselves on the huge "middle" class we have developed, but as Dr. John Raines of Temple University has recently pointed out, "There is not so much a middle class as a class at the top and a class made up of the rest of us who pay the bills. There is less middle class affluence than middle class moonlighting, worry and exhaustion." He notes that in 1949 1 percent of our population owned 21 percent of the nation's personal wealth. In 1959 it was 30 percent and in 1969, 40 percent. It is, of course, tax laws that favor the wealthy which enable them to continue accumulating riches.

At the same time, however, an unexpected malaise of discontent has settled over many a "winner" who has achieved his goals: made his money, reached status, fulfilled his dreams. "Is this all there is to it?" he asks. "Was it worth the price I paid to get here?"

Nowhere is this discontent more clearly reflected than in a recent survey of businessmen by the American Management Association. Polling 7,200 "management persons" as to their ideas of success, they received 2,821 thoughtful replies, the highest response to a survey in the fifty-year history of AMA research. (The results, published in 1973 as "The Changing Success Ethic," are available from the AMA, 135 W. 50th St., New York, N.Y., for $7.50.)

Here are some of the conclusions. Seventy percent of the respondents are unhappy in what they are doing and would like to make a change. Half have already changed their line of work. More than half face pressures to conform to standards which make them uncomfortable. Almost one-third feel that job requirements have adversely affected their health. And most of them have come to a new definition of success. It has less to do with material well-being and more to do with "the richness of human experience and opportunity for true self-expression."

If success is thought of as "achieving a goal," both the goal and the idea of achieving it are changing. For many, simply the sense of inner satisfaction of being in a process of growth is sufficient to spell success, whether or not one ever "arrives." The goal has less to do with external standards imposed by society, more to do with one's own inner desires. In many cases it involves a desire to strengthen one's spiritual roots.

Those who feel themselves successful share several tendencies, these among them: to hold religious faith and values, to exalt qualities of personal integrity over "personality," to believe that good working relationships with subordinates are more important than pleasing the boss, and to view the disenchantment of youth as symptomatic of an ethical breakdown in American society.

I tested these propositions recently at a conference of Christian workers and found it to be especially true of men and women who have undergone a profound Christian experience. "What is success?" I asked. "Have your ideas changed over the years? And do you feel successful today?" Here are some of the answers I got.

Dave Stoner, Jacksonville, Fla.: The shape of success for me comes from being in the midst of something that has meaning at an emotional level, to feel good about me and what I am doing. At one time I was totally materialistic. One of my goals was to make a lot of money and have a lot of power in a community where my opinions meant something. The change came when that to which I was committed changed. When I could really believe and begin to own, even in a very small measure, God's love for me, my ideas began to change. I have short-range goals now. I have no goals for five years from now, or even next year. Whatever it is that I'm about, I want to feel good about it. Being has taken the place of having and doing. And I feel successful, I really do.

Margaret Everett, Pittsburgh, Pennsylvania: I once thought success was accomplishing something significant, being the best in whatever I set out to do. Now I think of it more in terms of being the best kind of person I can be. How can I be maximum? I still have long-term goals, but the important question I ask myself is, "How am I?" Are all the parts of my life integrated to make a workable whole? I feel more successful than, say, three years ago. But I keep finding areas that aren't well integrated and still need working on.

Clif Cartland, Glendale, California: Success has become more internal than external. Growing up, it was having a car of my own, having enough money so you didn't have to count pennies at the end of the month. Today I feel successful when I'm accomplishing some internal goal, such as being aware of my feelings and acting on them rather than swallowing them.

I went through an "achievement motivation process" one week where we had to identify several successful experiences in each period of our lives. My first reaction was that I hadn't had any. But as I thought in terms of what made me feel good, I realized that I had had lots of them. I felt successful when I was recognized publicly, when I was thought of as a professional. That's still part of me. I haven't tried to change it. I can say, "O.K., that's what's inside of me." But it's growth to recognize it and not be hung up on it. Growth is what I'm after, emotional and spiritual growth. I used to see them as separate but not any more. Spiritual growth involves healthy emotional growth.

Gary Howell, Mason City, Iowa: Most of us who profess Christianity are striving toward wholeness. My idea of success is a feeling of O.K.ness in the midst of that striving. I can't say that I've reached wholeness; however, I feel a lot better about myself now than I did a few years ago. To me, that's success.

I am a product of the depression years. I grew up feeling the male's role is to provide for his family, so success focused on how well I did financially and that depended on making progress in business. Recently I've turned down opportunities to move up in my company. The job I now have allows time for my family and for personal growth and ministry. The one I could have had would have eliminated much of this. So, for me, success is also having the courage to allow God to guide my decisions concerning my vocational progress.

Morgan Williams, Topeka, Kansas: My idea of success has changed. At one time it meant becoming a leader, being respected in the community, having power, being part of the power structure so that you could make decisions and change things. Well, I became a community leader, a part of the power structure. I was disillusioned about my ability to bring about constructive change. I found that the things I really wanted to do were not possible until I worked on my own personal freedom. So I had to back up, retreat and lead with my own personhood before I could move out into the world and be successful in the organization of which I am a part.

Today success means living out my talents with people on a one-to-one basis and in small groups to try to bring change. I also need to be part of a larger movement or organization, but I find that without the personal, the other becomes meaningless; and without the larger thing, my personal search becomes ingrown.

ᑎᑌ᙭ᑎᔕ

These answers from people at the conference confirm two interesting findings that stand out in the comments made by businessmen in response to the AMA survey. One echoes a pungent statement in Huber's book: "Success is not a harbor but a voyage. . . . The lesson that most of us on this voyage never learn, but can never quite forget, is that *to win is sometimes to lose.*" The late Alan Watts spoke of this in a wider context when he summarized much of the recent history of our nation as "the failure of success in America."

The other truth is the converse of the first: *to lose is sometimes to win.* As Samuel Smiles puts it in *Self-Help* (Transatlantic, 1959), "We learn from failure much more than from success." Perhaps failure, or a certain degree of it, is almost a precondition of success, if we can see the failure as a stepping stone to personal spiritual growth.

What has been your experience? Does it echo these sentiments? Or does it differ in some substantial way? Have your goals changed through the process of everyday living? Has spiritual growth altered your concept of success?

Success has so many facets. *Is our nation succeeding,* for instance? We are experiencing a good deal of failure but perhaps in the long run our present crises will be seen as turning points toward a new and higher morality.

Our age of innocence as a nation is certainly over. We are like all other people after all—no better and no worse. More blessed, perhaps, than most, but with no overabundance of morality and just as much in need of God's grace. Our greatest loss may be our pride, but perhaps we will someday say—as the aftershave commercial puts it, "Thanks! We needed that!"

Was Jesus a success? Now there's an intriguing question, whether you put it in the past tense and ask it about Jesus of Nazareth, or put it in the present tense and ask it about the success of his enterprise today. A friend of mine—in answer to the present tense form of the question—says, "It's too soon to tell." But I'm inclined to answer it—in both its forms—with another question: "By whose standards?"

Success, after all, can only be measured by the goals set for it. So what were (and are) Jesus' goals? It seems safe to say that Jesus of Nazareth did not value a single one of the success-goals so constantly held up to us as Americans: status, affluence, comfort—you name it.

As far as we know, he never owned a house, had a family,

held a high-paying job, built up a bank account, held high office. And he certainly didn't live to a ripe old age. Jesus did, in fact, have very different standards and he found it extremely difficult to explain them, even to his confidants.

"The Son of Man did not come to be served," he said; "he came to serve and to give his life to redeem many people" (Mark 10:45, TEV). That's a far cry from such modern goals as making sure my needs are met, finding out who I am, or loving and serving myself.

And what response did Jesus get? Just what you might expect. Peter began to rebuke him when Jesus foretold his rejection and death. No one understood or accepted this. "He was despised and rejected . . . , a man of sorrows, and acquainted with grief," as the prophet Isaiah predicted (53:3).

But he was also successful. In Isaiah's words, "He shall see the fruit of the travail of his soul and be satisfied" (53:11). The writer to the Hebrews calls Jesus "the pioneer and perfector of our faith, who for the joy that was set before him endured the cross, despising the shame" (Heb. 12:2). Out of seeming failure came success and it was worth it.

Are you a success? How do you feel about where you are right now? Are you where you would like to be? Are you at least in process—with the resources and support system—feeling you are growing in the right direction?

There are discoveries for you—for all of us. One of them is that in Jesus' way death precedes resurrection. The way up is the way down, to use Fritz Kunkel's phrase. "God's strength is made perfect in weakness."

And there are things you can do. Destructive processes can be slowed to a halt. Bad situations can be faced. Risks can be taken, adventures begun. It's amazing how much can flow from one courageous step of faith taken right now.

I hope the material that follows helps you take that step.

WINNING ISN'T EVERYTHING

George B. Leonard

The time has come, argues George B. Leonard, in this
address at the Esalen Sports Symposium, to blow the
whistle on madness that produces not winners but
losers . . . conformists . . . a nightmare of life without
ultimate meaning.

This important article is reprinted by permission from
Intellectual Digest, October 1973. Copyright © 1973 by
Communications/Research/Machines, Inc.

In less than a generation, the prevailing sports ethos in
America has shifted from "It's not whether you win or lose, it's
how you play the game" to "Winning isn't everything—it's the
only thing."

The current public glorification of winning at all costs came
to the fore during a war we did not win. Sermons by top corporate executives on hot competition as the American way
were being directed at the younger generation during a period
when many of these same executives were making every
effort to get around the federal regulations against price-fixing
and illegal cooperation among corporate "competitors." The
use of sports terminology by our national administration became commonplace just before the nation learned how misleading and disastrous "game plans" and "enemy lists" can
be. . . .

The attempt to justify hot competition as an essential aspect
of human existence goes on in the face of all the evidence.
There exists, for example, a common assumption that competition is needed to "motivate behavior." Yet no study has shown
that competition necessarily motivates behavior any more
effectively than other means—extrinsic reinforcement, for in-

stance, or even the sheer joy of doing something well. To see the real function of competition in our society, we must look deeper.

In 1967, I collaborated with Marshall McLuhan on an article entitled, "The Future of Education." Our idea sessions ranged over a number of topics but kept coming back to the question of competition and why it is so tirelessly proclaimed, not only by coaches, but by educators and all those traditionalists who concern themselves with shaping the lives of our young people. At last McLuhan came forth with one of his "probes"—a sudden thought from an unexpected direction.

"I know," he said; "competition creates resemblance."

To compete with someone, in other words, you must agree to run on the same track, to do what he is doing, to follow the same set of rules. The only way you'll differentiate yourself is by doing precisely the same thing, slightly faster or better. Thus, though performance may improve, the chances are you will become increasingly like the person with whom you compete.

In this light, it is easy to see that a culture dedicated to creating standardized, specialized, predictable human components could find no better way of grinding them out than by making every possible aspect of life a matter of competition. "Winning out" in this respect does not make rugged individualists. It shapes conformist robots. Keep your eyes open during the football season. The defensive ends begin to look more and more alike. The quarterbacks become ever more interchangeable.

The final argument for hot competition all the way down to nursery school is that competition makes winners. The argument is, at best, half true. It makes nonwinners, too—generally more nonwinners than winners. And a number of studies indicate that losing can become a lifelong habit. What is more, when competition reaches the present level, the argument becomes altogether false. As proclaimed by the more extreme coaches and sportswriters today, competition makes us—all of us—losers.

Between 1958 and 1971 the San Francisco Giants had the best overall won-lost record in the National League. For five straight years, from 1965 through 1969, they finished in second place. To do this, you would think, they must have "won out" over many other teams. Increasingly during this period of second-place finishes, however, they came to be characterized by fan and sportswriter alike as born losers.

"Winning isn't everything—it's the only thing." And in our present-day sports culture, that means being Number One, Numero Uno, the one and only.

Take the Dallas Cowboys. For five straight years, from 1966 through 1970, the Cowboys won their division championships, then were eliminated, either in the playoffs or finally, in January of 1971, in the Super Bowl itself. And what was said of this fine professional football team during this period of unprecedented winning? They "couldn't be the big ones." They were, you see, just losers.

When the Cowboys did at last win the Super Bowl, in January 1972, it became apparent that the players themselves had been swept up in the Numero Uno mystique. One by one they came to the TV camera after the game to affirm that nothing had really meant anything except this victory. The champagne flowed. The players were probably happy for a moment but their faces were not entirely unclouded. And the mask of fear that coach Tom Landry wears along the sidelines during every game when his winning record is threatened was not entirely erased. The problem is this: even after you've just won the Super Bowl—*especially* after you've just won the Super Bowl—*there's always next year.*

If there is truth in the statement, "Winning isn't everything —it's the only thing," then "the only thing" is nothing—emptiness, the nightmare of life without ultimate meaning. This emptiness pursues us wherever "winning out" is proclaimed as

God. I once spoke to a group of top-ranking industrialists in a seminar session and argued that hot competition is far from inevitable in the future. As my argument developed, I noticed a look of real anxiety on some of the faces around me. One industrialist finally spoke up, "If there is to be no competition, then what will life be all about?" We would probably be appalled to discover how many people in this culture have no notion of accomplishment for its own sake and define their own existence solely in terms of how many other people they can beat out.

There is nothing wrong with competition in the proper proportion. Like a little salt, it adds zest to the game and to life itself. But when the seasoning is mistaken for the substance, only sickness can follow. Similarly, when winning becomes "the only thing," it can lead only to eventual emptiness and anomie.

Blow the whistle on this madness. We may not be able to turn the American sports juggernaut around overnight, but we can suggest that sports are possible without beating the brains out of the opposing team, and that it may be possible for players and fans alike to take great pleasure in a beautiful play, even if it's executed by the opposition. We can start working out new sports that are noncompetitive or less competitive or in which competition is placed in the proper perspective, as a matter of good sport and good humor. We can start looking for the larger potentialities that actually already exist in the realm of sports and games.

Our present way of life, based upon endless, ever-increasing expansion of the production and consumption of energy, is eventually doomed. And so much else is based upon that expansion—our definition of job and full employment, our inculcation and suppression of aggression, our attempts to fix consciousness at a single point, our whole neurosis structure, our glorification of what we call "competition" and "winning." The present state of expansion in the United States can go on for a few more decades, but then it comes up against the most fundamental law of thermodynamics. Even with perfectly clean nuclear energy, the final result of all burning and wasteful consumption will be the overheating of this small planet. We must seek alternate modes of life, other ways of being on this earth.

Changes are coming. Sports represent a key joint in any society. To turn this society toward peaceful, humane change, we can begin with reform of sports. Some intellectuals have ignored this aspect of our life, believing somehow that sports are beyond serious consideration. They are quite mistaken. There is nothing trivial about the flight of a ball, for it traces for us the course of the planet. Through the movement of the human body, we can come to know what the philosopher Pythagoras called *kosmos,* a word containing the idea of both perfect order and intense beauty. Sports are too beautiful and profound for simplistic slogans. How we play the game may turn out to be more important than we imagine, for it signifies nothing less than our way of being in the world.

TAMING THE DRAGON

Sandy Welton

Success has been like a dragon to me—a beast to be tracked down and slain—or a beast to be avoided.

I grew up as one of America's overprivileged youth. My dad was a successful doctor, and my mom the adequate family developer. I had received a good education, had two older brothers to model after, a younger sister to take my aggressions out on and was generally encouraged to be whatever I wanted to be.

But no one's script is perfect. During my junior and senior high school years my parents struggled with the meaning of their marriage and whether or not they should continue it. This had a profound effect on me and I became more and more a loner and a questioner. The uncertainties of my home life were compounded by new ones elsewhere. I transferred to a new school in the eighth grade, losing much of my former status. I didn't make the football or basketball teams in the ninth grade (the cornerstones of my previous self-esteem) and I lost seven straight high school elections as a finalist for different offices.

It was during these years that I turned to Christianity as a source of security and identity. It provided me with assurance when there was very little I was sure of. Two basic goals were important to me: to become a successful and prosperous businessman and to be an active Christian witness. I was determined to fight through the pain and loneliness of life to reach

At the time he wrote this, Sandy Welton was studying clinical psychology at Southeast Institute, Chapel Hill, North Carolina.

24

these high plateaus where all strong and "normal" white males in our society belong.

Graduating from college in 1967 was no treat. Diplomas were anathema, as they had been transformed from tickets of success into tickets to Vietnam. I was against the war, though I didn't really know why. I was in no way a campus activist and my Christian faith had not sensitized me to social issues. I was a typical evangelical Christian who only knew that Jesus was the answer, no matter what the questions were.

But from somewhere within me I experienced a tremendous crisis in values. I was determined not to go to Vietnam, and my reasons had to do with Jesus Christ, though I had never really thought them through. Fortunately, I was able to get a job as a "Christian youth worker" in Atlanta, which was a way of doing alternative service and of giving me some thinking time.

Doing full time "Christian" work for low pay is one good way to spur a person on to read the Bible and check out exactly what Jesus said and meant. For me it was a way of making the Sermon on the Mount more than a set of spiritual goodies. Gradually I found my traditional views of life eroding under that sermon and a flood of new experiences. With Vietnam as a starter, I began to question almost everything in sight. I was hearing drum beats I didn't know existed, wishing they would go away, yet listening at the same time.

Christianity became quite a problem to me. As I grew in my anger toward the war and toward unjust social conditions in America, I became more and more frustrated at the degree to which Christianity was captive to American policy. Especially disappointing to me was evangelical Christianity. That segment of the church seemed blind to the corporate responsibilities of faith. Saying no to Caesar, peacemaking and sharing appeared to be concepts lost in history.

In fear and trembling I began to give up my original goals, first my goal of becoming a successful businessman and then my goal of becoming a successful Christian evangelist. That was quite a sacrifice (and guilt trip) because I grew up in Billy Graham's hometown and had calculated that I might make an excellent replacement (the age difference was just about right) for Mr. Graham. But give it up I did. I no longer knew if Jesus was the answer, though he did strike me as posing a pretty good question.

With my former script in shambles, I was in need of developing a new plan for my life. I continued to want to define my life in some Christian sense, but it had to be one that reflected a sense of integrity with regard to social problems. I found a new home in what is commonly referred to as the "radical Christian community"—a group of people who see in Jesus a liberator of oppressed people. Being Christian was, in part, being a constructive agitator and hopefully a reconciler. Because of Vietnam and the plight of America's poor (two of many issues), the responsibility of the Christian needed to include active protest against the inhumanity of present conditions and work for new conditions. Thus, my choice was to continue asking and experimenting to find new ways of demonstrating spiritual truths in human terms.

My efforts within this framework have been extensive over the last four years. I have been a part of a number of successful efforts to stage reasonable protests and imaginative actions for correcting unjust social conditions. Yet I must admit I do not feel very successful. The problems have been too staggering and the opposing forces too great. My idealism of four years ago has been modified by many harsh experiences and the "cold facts" of our adult world. I recently told a professor at Duke University that I was suffering from "apocalyptic depression."

So where am I? I am not the successful politician I had dreamed about in childhood. Nor a successful businessman. Nor a successful Christian evangelist. And not even a successful "radical."

Yet I am happier and more full of life than ever before. The last year has been one in which I have learned to celebrate my own being and enjoy others. Some synthesis has come about with all the changes I have gone through. I now see my initial growth from being a traditional evangelical Christian to a radical Christian was not growth at all; it was comparable to a baby switching from his or her mother's right breast to her (far) left breast. With this insight, I can't say I've lost my interest in breasts, but I can say I no longer need a dogma—be it left or right, Christian or non-Christian—to justify my worth as a person and make my life worthwhile.

I have fallen in love with my capacity to change what I don't like about my own life and increase what I do like. I have begun to really enjoy my own self and if I understand the gospel's story about God Immanuel correctly, that is spiritual maturity.

My search for success is no longer a search, really; it is a happening. It is not a static goal to be reached at age forty, fifty, or sixty, but a process, a way of life, presently taking place. I experience it when I act as a responsible adult, owning my body, thoughts, desires, words, actions and feelings. I am successful as I allow myself to become all that I have the capacity to become. I experience success as I am open to others and become a person with whom they can share the full range of human emotions. To me, this is humanizing the ideas of success, because it is potentially available to all people at all ages.

I am presently confused about what to do beyond the boundaries of my own well-being. If the activism of the sixties has ceased, the problems have not. They have done little more than surface. So, for me, success needs to include not only experiencing a meaningful life as an individual but also living responsibly as a corporate member of our society. For males born into white upper-middle-class society, this poses quite a challenge. How do I rework my self-image and being so that I both affirm myself and the other members of humanity?

This, to me, strikes at the taproot of repentance, *metanoia,* as Jesus spoke of it. It is to become a new person, not only in an individual spiritual or emotional sense, but in a corporate sense. It is to take America's poor or Vietnam's refugees seriously by growing into a new consciousness of human partnership that goes beyond the boundaries of laissez-faire capitalism. It is to rework my values, my lifestyles and my social energy to create a new corporate happening.

Success is a word and a concept we all must live with. It's that American. But it doesn't have to be a dragon either to be slain or to be avoided. Each of us has the power to redefine it and humanize it. Besides, I've never seen this dragon. For all I know it's a myth.

IT'S O.K. TO BE SUCCESSFUL

Mark Henry

For most of my life, the only Christian witnesses I heard were of dramatic, life-saving conversions. For some it was from drugs or drink. For others it was from the rejection of family and friends, or perhaps self-rejection. Whatever the reason, the path led to a messed-up life, all too often to mental and even physical suicide. But turning to God, they found hope and a way back.

While I accept the reality of these, I find them difficult to relate to. My life has been great, successful and happy. Failure is not easy for me to understand, because I haven't experienced much of it.

I began to wonder if I would have to have a crash-and-burn, face-in-the-mud experience to be a real Christian. I asked God if it had to be that way, because I wasn't sure I wanted any part of it.

God's response was loud and clear. He accepts me as I am. I don't have to apologize for being successful. I don't have to try to top each success with a bigger and better one. God has a unique purpose for me and that gives me the freedom to work and live my life.

For a while I felt that being a full-time Christian meant professional church work. I felt sure I was to give up my comfortable, middle income life and become a minister or a church administrator. I pursued that, but no doors opened. I am convinced that God wants me where I am, working at TRW, being his person on the job. He wants me leading small groups,

Mark Henry is manager of business planning and control at TRW Systems, Houston Operations, and lives in Seabrook, Texas.

enabling others to experience meaningful relationships both with each other and with him. In my life, work, family and relationships, he wants me to be the person he created me to be. If that is a successful, leader-type person, then I am free to enjoy it and praise him for it.

Being successful does not mean perfection. I am human. But I get uptight when I hear someone say about themselves that they are worthless, nothing. I read somewhere that "God don't make no junk."* I believe that. Each of us has worth and value simply because he created us, even if we don't recognize him or accept him. But only when we accept him and ask for his guidance can we reach or even approach the potential he has for us.

---

*From Herbert B. Barks, Jr., *Words Are No Good If the Game Is Solitaire* (Waco, Texas: Word Books, 1971), p. 56, quoted on the front cover of FAITH/AT/WORK, April 1972.

EXPERIENTIAL EXERCISES

The exercises which follow and those that appear at the end of each chapter in this book may be used either as an individual discipline or as part of a group experience. If done in a group, you may want to select only those exercises that seem most suited to the people who will be engaged in the process.

Exercise 1. Close your eyes, relax, and project a fantasy of being on a journey that will carry you five years into your personal future. Imagine God opening doors for you along the journey. This journey is to lead to your becoming the most complete person you are capable of being. You are to move into fulfillment and happiness as you move toward your future. Allow five to ten minutes for silent reflection on such a journey, then describe your journey to two other persons. Let them help you clarify the dream. Listen to their dreams and ask questions or make observations that will help them clarify their journeys. After all have shared their dreams, individually make a list of the things that you would need to do now to start moving toward the fulfillment of your dream.

Exercise 2. Identify three occasions during the past year when you felt successful. Write these down. Reflect on what they have in common, if anything. It may be helpful to distinguish which were accomplishments or achievements that brought internal satisfaction, which were victories resulting from competition observable to any who could have seen you succeed. Share with others in your group either an accomplishment or victory that you have experienced in this past year.

Exercise 3. Reflect on the way in which you employ your time. Write down the five things that take most of your time and energy. Explain to another person what the end result would be of being able to do each of these five things well. Ask yourself the question, "Would being able to do the things I do now very well spell success?"

31

Exercise 4. On each of ten cards or pieces of paper, write a different statement that begins. "I am _____." Number these ten statements in the order of their importance to you right now. Share with the group or with one other person which three of these "I am" statements you could discard from your life with the least pain or regret. After sharing and hearing each others' lists, share which three of the statements are the most important to you right now. Do these represent success?

Exercise 5. Looking back over your entire life, think of several successes you have experienced. Which of these successes or victories are still successes today, and which have faded or become unimportant to you now? Share with another person why the success that has faded was important to you at the time and why you feel it is not important now. Next, share which success is still an important part of your life today and why.

2.
POWER

Coming to Terms with Power

IS POWER a dirty word?

Many people shun the idea of power as something evil, though they may at the same time seek it surreptitiously. As psychologist Rollo May puts it, "Power is widely coveted and rarely admitted." To admit to wanting power is an action some of us cannot allow ourselves. The reasons are several.

"Power corrupts." All of us have heard that familiar dictum, and it is true. We distrust, therefore, the accumulation of power by others and try to put ourselves in a good light by disallowing our own drive for power. But giving up power is no answer.

Powerlessness corrupts too. It is the lack of power that produces the frustration that ultimately leads to violence. Who wants to be powerless?

Do you remember the last time you felt powerless? Take a minute to recall the occasion. Where were you and when? What was happening around you? In what way did you experience the lack of power? How did it feel?

Three groups of people, at least, eschew power: the sick, the disillusioned, and the religious.

The ill—both mentally and physically—who crowd our institutions include among them a sizable number of people who do not want to take responsibility for themselves and—either consciously or unconsciously—render themselves sick and powerless, turning the responsibility for their care over to others.

The disillusioned can be seen on every hand—from those "straight people" who were so affronted by recent abuses of political power that they have declared a pox on all politicians, to the young in the counterculture who, in rebelling against technology and the conventional "work ethic," have dropped out to live off the land or off gratuitous handouts. They renounce the drive for power and pretend to live as if power is altogether evil. Rollo May calls their hideout *pseudo-innocence,* a cop-out on their responsibility as human beings rather than the return to innocence they suppose it to be.

But the religious—among them many Christians—may well form the largest group of dropouts. "I live by love, not power," they say, as if one can be set over against the other. But love is a form of power, perhaps the most powerful of all forms of power.

These people deceive themselves even as they try to fool others. Their drive for power goes underground, sometimes wearing a pious disguise. Confronted with any accomplishment, some Christians take refuge behind a denial of any personal instrumentality. "I didn't do it," they say; "it was the Lord."

ᗡᖇᗡ

But *power* is not a dirty word, and the sooner we recognize that fact the better. It is a necessity of life. The word itself means *ability,* and goes back to the Latin *passe,* to be able. And what's wrong with being able?

Every person, in order to esteem himself, must have a certain degree of power. Even newborn babies are not totally powerless. They have the power to cry, and with that they begin to assert themselves in the world.

Power is necessary for any achievement, for communication,

for love, for ethical action. Power exists in every human relationship; in fact, its dynamic is what describes the nature of the relationship. Power is needed to influence others, for good as well as for evil. And who does not want to have an influence for good? One cannot care for others or be helpful to them without acting out of some sense of one's own identity and worth. That spells p-o-w-e-r.

⁓⁓⁓

Power is a very Christian word. And more and more Christians are recognizing its validity. God is the source of power. "Thine is the . . . power and the glory," we remind ourselves as we worship. God gives power to the faint. His power is made perfect in weakness. The cross of Christ is the power of God to salvation. "You shall receive power when the Holy Spirit has come upon you," Jesus promised. (See Matt. 6:13; Isa. 40:20; 2 Cor. 12:9; Rom. 1:16; 1 Cor. 1:17–18; Acts 1:8.) The good news is not that we are powerless or that God would render us powerless so that he can shine in contrast to us. It is an offer of power: "To all who received him . . . he gave power to become children of God" (John 1:12).

So we mustn't minimize our power. We must accept what we have and seek to use it for good. God's gift of power is to be accepted, to be owned as our own. It is not to be denied, nor to be hid from behind pious phrases.

But we must not make power our *ultimate* aim. Power should always be sought for some other purpose, not simply for its own sake. Power needs to serve the ends of justice and love.

The most powerful power, perhaps, is that which comes without being sought. Is this what Jesus meant when he said, "Blessed are the meek, for they shall inherit the earth" (Matt. 5:5)? Meekness is the quality that does not seek power for its own sake and which, as a result, accrues to itself a depth of integrity. "But seek ye first the kingdom of God, and his righteousness," Jesus concluded, "and all these things shall be added unto you" (Matt. 6:33, KJV).

He who would rightly use power must be committed to

something beyond power and must be able also to submit to the power of others when he is called to live and work under their authority.

❧❧❧

Power must be analyzed with discernment. There are different kinds of power, as well as different degrees of it. In his outstanding book *Power and Innocence* (Norton, 1972), Rollo May makes some valuable distinctions. He differentiates, first of all, five levels of power.

First is the *power to be,* that power that is central in every infant's development through childhood to adulthood. Second is *self-affirmation,* the cry for recognition and significance that is the heart of psychological health. Third is *self-assertion,* a stronger, more overt behavior that determines how we respond to challenge and attack. Fourth is *aggression,* a stronger reaction still that develops when we are blocked or oppressed over a period of time. Finally, *violence* is the ultimate explosion of pent-up power against frustration and suppression.

May also distinguishes five kinds of power. Beginning at the destructive end of the spectrum, he speaks of that which is *exploitative,* which subjects persons to slavery and abuse. *Manipulative* power is power over a person—differing from exploitative power as a con man differs from a gun man—but still using people as if they were "things." *Competitive* power is power *against* another and embraces both the destructive possibility of putting someone else down as you move up, or the constructive drawing out of unused capabilities by both parties to the competition. *Nutrient* power is power *for* a person, "the power that is given by one's care for the other." Finally, there is *integrative* power, which is power *with* the other person, the power that stands alongside the other, supporting, aiding and abetting his/her efforts, contributing to his/her growth and effectiveness.

All of us distinguish different "currencies of power": political power, the power of money, physical power, the power of personality, of character, of conviction, of faith, of prayer.

Is there such a thing as spiritual power divorced from physical properties or human embodiment? What is the power of the Holy Spirit that God promises as his gift? What is the power of prayer?

Does love have power? Opinions on that question cover the spectrum from those who insist that love is the greatest power in the world to those who see it as the opposite of power. In Rollo May's words, "Power is seen as loveless and love as powerless."

Two things have happened to me in the process of thinking through this topic. I've come in touch with power I didn't know I had, and that's good. I've also discovered how uncomfortable I have been much of my life with the idea of power, and that's not so good.

If you're caught in the same predicament I have been in, I'd like to spare you some of the trouble I've been through. I have spent far too much time—from early childhood until now— feeling powerless. Was it because I was sickly as a child? Was it because I was the youngest and smallest boy in my class? Was it because the Quaker home in which I was reared urged silence at the dinner table and frowned on fighting and on all loud expressions of feeling? Was it a Christian theology that ascribed virtue to the kind of self-denial that puts oneself down as a worm or a doormat?

Whatever the reason, I felt powerless much of the time. But my dreams gave me away. Night after night I dreamed I was pursued by some ugly force only to find myself unable to resist or run away. I can remember waking up time after time from this recurrent dream frozen in my tracks and hating it. Outwardly, I was a "nice guy" and set about making everybody like me, rarely daring to stick up for myself or go against the crowd. At the same time I retreated into daydreams to "get even" with those who were bigger than I and who were obviously mistreating me.

So it has been good for me to wrestle with the theme of power. I dislike the way I have lived, now that I am aware of it, and have consciously set out on another course.

All around me I see people trapped in powerlessness—though they don't need to be—and I want to shout, "Wake up! You've got more power than you know. And it's O.K., God gave it to you and intends for you to use it."

This is clear to me from the Bible, beginning with the first commandment God gave man: "Be fruitful and multiply, and fill the earth and subdue it; and *have dominion over* . . . every living thing that moves upon the earth" (Gen. 1:28).

Power is a gift from God. Of course, he sets limits within which it is to be used—ethical and moral limits. God's intention was that man remain under the divine dominion while he exercised his own. To handle well one's own authority (another word for power), one needs to submit to God's authority. But man rebels at the idea.

It is easy for power to go to one's head, and I am troubled by the abuses that it can lead to. They are all too obvious in politics and business; they are more subtle in Christian circles. There is the "star system" which elevates certain individuals—because they are athletes or entertainers, because they have charisma or have written a sensational book—to positions where they can bask in the adulation of their followers.

But the fault is not all theirs. We contribute to their illusion of power by denying our own. We are willing to follow Pied Pipers rather than do our own hard thinking. We prefer being mice to men.

There are subtler dangers. They can happen in a sharing group or at a conference. In sharing our problems we can be manipulated. Describe a difficulty and you may get a Band-Aid instead of real help. Your sharing may bring a Scripture verse tossed your way, the suggestion that you "pray about it," or some advice in which you feel the pressure to be what someone else wants you to be rather than allow you to be yourself.

Don't misunderstand me. There's a time to quote Scripture and a time to pray. But there's a time not to, as well. When we do it to avoid sensitive listening to another's problem and the attendant discomfort we may feel, we're Band-Aiding.

But there's a deeper issue at stake. We allow these things to happen by giving away our power. We accept advice all too readily. We *let* ourselves be Band-Aided.

The next time it happens to you—and you're aware of it— say forthrightly, "I don't find that helpful," and ask for the help you need. Stick up for yourself. Don't let yourself be discounted or manipulated. You deserve to be taken seriously. You have the power to make up your mind and act on your decisions. You also have the right to ask for help, and the power to decide whether or not it is helpful.

The Apostle Paul makes a surprising statement in 1 Corinthians 4:20: "The kingdom of God does not consist in talk but in *power.*" You have more power than you know. If you are Christ's, the Holy Spirit dwells in you to give wisdom, grace and guidance—all you need for living.

I hope you'll get more in touch with your own power. Find your gifts and develop them. Think through your faith and validate what's real in your experience. Find what God wants you to do and do it. Be the person God intends you to be. That way lies true freedom and responsible living.

Perhaps you'll find help in what Harold Hughes and Karl Olsson have to say on the subject.

TWO KINDS OF POWER

Harold Hughes

Harold Hughes, for three terms governor of Iowa and for six years a United States Senator, left office in 1975, voluntarily relinquishing the political power that kept him in the spotlight of public acclaim for more than a decade.

It was not clear as yet—even to the senator—what he would be doing in the future, though the influences of the Prayer Group Movement in Washington, D.C., on his Christian commitment presaged that his energies would be directed to expanding their influence and seeking to lead men and women in positions of leadership to consider the spiritual ends of life.

It is not often that politicians voluntarily leave office to go into the Lord's work. For that reason FAITH/ AT/WORK editors interviewed Senator Hughes to discuss the motivation behind his decision. In what follows we share with you the larger part of that interview held in mid-October, 1974.

FAW: You are about to give up political power. Have you found a greater power you want to exercise?

Hughes: I'm not giving up any power. I've enjoyed my years in political office, but I don't look at working for the Lord full time as giving up power. I think that's the greatest power in creation and so, to me, I'm not giving up power. I rely on the Lord and his strength rather than my own strength and the political processes of this country.

FAW: There are different kinds of power then?

Hughes: There are different kinds. Sometimes they run along parallel lines and sometimes they have similar goals, but certainly there are different kinds when we think of eternal life as compared to political success in this material world.

FAW: So it's a matter of goals?

Hughes: It's a matter of realizing that, ultimately, you really believe the Word of God as set down in the Bible and your commitment to that Word. If you really believe in Jesus Christ and him crucified and the Word he has given us to live by, the final decision-making process has to be to do all we can to further his kingdom and prepare the way and establish it.

Since I committed my life to Christ twenty years ago, I have been led in ways that seem miraculous. In 1973 I suddenly realized that if I ran for reelection and won, it would commit me to another six years in office and that would bring me to an age where I would not be able to do some of the other things I want to do. I think the world is getting increasingly more troubled because of spiritual emptiness in the hearts of the people and the hearts of the leaders of the world.

FAW: And those are issues that can't be effectively dealt with through the political process?

Hughes: No. I think men have to come to Christ. He has the answers. And you can't alter the hearts of men by political activities. You can pass laws but you can't bring people to alter the nature of their being and their moral purpose.

FAW: Do you feel as strongly today about your decision to leave office as you did when you announced it over a year ago?

Hughes: I feel more strongly than ever. The decision has been affirmed by God many times since I announced it and I'm looking forward to the time when my service in the Senate ends and I can begin to unwind a lot of things that I think need unwinding in myself. I want to spend time in thought and meditation and prayer, reading the Word and starting to feel myself as something other than the political animal I have been for a lot of years.

I've attempted to use God's guidance in my political career —not all the time, but much of the time. Sometimes I've found myself not making the right decision, and almost always it's been when I wasn't turning to God but making the decision on my own intellect and emotions. I was trying to *be* God in the political process rather than *let* God help me.

FAW: What confirmations of your decision are you referring to?

Hughes: They've come in every way you can imagine. Experiences I've had with people, invitations, seeing people commit their lives to Christ, or recommit them and make drastic changes in their thinking. They've come in revelation to people in prayer groups, in opportunities that have opened up for me to witness that couldn't have come in any other way, in people who have come to me for counseling and advice as a result of the decision being made public. Many thousands of people have responded to my decision positively, and that, to me, is a reflection both of the will of God in my decision and of the hunger in the hearts of men and women, not only in this country but all around the world.

FAW: Are you less interested now in the social concerns you've always been involved in, Senator?

Hughes: The intensity of my interest in social problems and the needs of people is as great as it ever was, though I may look at them in a little different light now. The last three years, particularly, have intensified the depth of my thinking about social programs. I'm not sure that over the years—in my sixteen years of public life—I have really tried to determine the spiritual impact of programs on people as well as the material impact.

FAW: How do you feel about the use of power itself?

Hughes: I think it's one of the most difficult things in creation to handle. Power creates feelings that almost destroy humility, that build the ego, and that cause other people who are seeking something to do obeisance to the one who holds power, to bow down, to curtsy, and be willing to be led by the hand everywhere they go. Power makes a person feel kingly. Suddenly one finds himself feeling that he's entitled to the position, that he is, as a matter of fact, better than other people. The power syndrome is dangerous.

Power is hard to give up. I think this is what makes wealth so difficult to manage. It gives one power, it becomes a great love, and it's very difficult to give up. I think anything you can't give up easily becomes a threat to your spiritual life. Christ said we should be willing to surrender all things for him, and power and money are very difficult to surrender.

FAW: If you don't mind our saying so, you're a very powerful person, Senator, in your physical bearing and forceful personality, and you have a moral power that everyone who knows you recognizes. How do you feel about that?

Hughes: It troubles me. I don't think I'm worthy of any of it. I know that my thoughts and actions require constant care in prayer and self-discipline that God may give me a clean mind and a clean tongue and a clean body and a clean heart.

If I were not aware of my temptations and my failures in the past, perhaps I could accept your statement more graciously. But if people see me as strong, it is because I am aware of my weaknesses. I am in need of Christ's strength constantly to sustain me. Alone I haven't any strength at all.

THE POWER TO BE AND TO BLESS

Karl Olsson

Christians normally don't talk much about power except in the context of "the power of God" or "the power of the Spirit," and I think it is high time for us to look at power in a more earthly way. All of us are involved in a power struggle of sorts. When decisions have to be made, power comes into play. The morally responsible use of power in all of our relationships is hence a needful task and we need to learn to do it well.

But although I am committed to the wise use of social power, I am going to come at power from a different angle. I want to affirm a kind of power which eluded me for many years and is just now becoming real.

For as long as I can remember, Romans 7 has been exposited in our Lutheran faith circles as argument for the powerlessness of Christians. This moving and very personal word of the Apostle Paul has shown us as prisoners to the law of sin which is at work in our bodies. Put simply, this has meant that we know what we ought to do but can't do it. Our despair over our inability provides an opportunity for grace. "Thanks be to God," exclaims Paul, "[I can be delivered from my imprisonment] through Jesus Christ our Lord!" (Rom. 7:25).

There is nothing in the theology of this passage with which I now disagree. I believe, as strongly as ever, that all of us struggle with a twistedness in our natures which makes us do things we do not want to do and prevents our doing what we want to do. I believe that we are prisoners of this twistedness and that nothing we can initiate in and of ourselves frees us.

Karl Olsson is the former director of leadership training for Faith at Work, and lives in Columbia, Maryland.

I also believe that only grace gives us the power to become and to be free people and communicators of the blessing.

How then does my present reading of Romans 7 differ from my previous one? I believe that sin binds us and grace frees us. I have always believed that. So what's new?

The new thing is my understanding and experience of grace. In talking about that I am going to be very personal.

There was a time when I preached on the new life in Christ and on the relationships which grow out of that life with an intensity which left me physically and emotionally exhausted. My special thing was the love of Christ which has been "shed abroad in our hearts." I saw Dostoyevsky's "active love" as the lifestyle I wanted for myself. I longed for the dynamic charity of Jesus, Paul, Father Zossima; I wanted to find the mystical quality of fellowship which Berdyaev talks about; the oneness with the other which leaps out like a flame without coercion or self-seeking.

But while I was talking about these things, I knew that they were unattainable. I came out of the pulpit guilty and ashamed because I had left my hearers, with myself, in an exalted despair which might be dissipated by the Sunday roast and the afternoon football game but which left us essentially where we had been. Grace hovered above us like a sunburst in a baroque church but we were left despondent down below, redeemed only in hope. It was as if we were prisoners whose days were made tolerable by a promise of liberation but who did not taste freedom.

I had visions of my sermons left carelessly by my listeners in the pews together with the mimeographed bulletins. Worse yet, I saw my sermon unheeded within myself. I felt robbed of the power to do what I so earnestly desired. I had held up the banner of active love, but I did not actively love many people. Once my system was stabilized and my blood pressure back to normal, I wanted to get away from what I had said, not because it was false but because I had no way of empowering it. In a curious way, the word remained with me sterile.

I am sure there are those who read my words as a put-down of all preaching and of me personally. I intend neither. I do not want to discredit the preaching of the Word or the Word itself. Nor do I want to luxuriate in self-contempt. I am talking only about my feelings when I came down from the pulpit and felt that I had completed a performance without empowering people.

The first difficulty, I am certain, was that I did not believe that grace was a process available to me through people. I was like the prisoner who thinks that his deliverance must come from a helicopter and not from tunneling through a wall. I was hollow, dissatisfied, guilty about the gap between my proclamation and my behavior, but I did not have the freedom to tell anyone. I waited greedily for the words of reassurance at the church door (o marketplace of false comforts!), but I would probably have flipped if someone had said, "I sense some pain in you. Is there something you would like to be free to share?"

But, of course, that was precisely my problem, or at least part of it. Unlike the Apostle Paul, I could not cry out, "I am miserable. Won't someone help me?" I didn't know I needed help. I didn't know where such help was available. I saw the whole thing as a theological problem, grave and perplexing to Paul, Augustine, Luther, Barth and all the smaller potatoes. Who was I to ask to be delivered from a pain borne with fortitude by these giants?

The second difficulty was that I failed to see that the grace process first of all had to bring me to love myself, to delight in myself. Such self-love and self-acceptance have nothing to do with the garden variety of egotism of which I had a large store and still do. I knew I was an egotist; hence I concluded that what I needed least was the power to love myself more and delight in myself more. But, of course, I was wrong. What I needed most was to be assured that I mattered. It was the suspicion that I did not which drove me to flagellate myself and others with all those sermons about active love.

The third difficulty was that I could not see that when Paul thanks God for the freeing grace available to him through Jesus, he is not talking merely about the transcendent Lord but about the Lord immanent in and indwelling his people. So that if I want to narrow and occasionally eliminate the gap between what I want to do and my ability to do it, the power to do that is available "where two or three are gathered in his name." There is, in other words, a way of being enabled and enabling others to do more than agonize about active love. There is power to love.

My three difficulties can hence be restated as three positive steps toward the power to be and to bless (enable).

1. The first step is to give up the fruitless monologue which sets me apart from the Lord's people and to share with them in groups of appropriate size both my joy and my misery. James 5:16 talks about confessing our sins to one another that we may be healed, but I believe that we need to expand the spectrum of sharing to all our concerns. Some things we may want to share with only one other; other things we may want to offer to a whole assembly.

2. The second step to power is to let the fellowship delight in my "me-ness" and to love me into loving myself. I think that this is the context in which *agape* love is meaningful. Delighting in myself does not mean that I select my good points or even my gifts as the focus of love. Delighting in myself means being grateful for my total identity—my awesome and ludicrous being which, we are assured, carries the divine image even when I have egg on my face.

3. The third step to power is, together with the fellowship and in the Spirit, to discover gifts of ministry in myself and others, and to free these gifts up to heal, bless and save people. This assignment sounds arrogant unless we see it as empowered by the Spirit. His power is our power. "To all who received him, who believed in his name, he gave power to become children of God; who were born, not of blood nor of the will of the flesh nor of the will of man, but of God" (John 1:12, 13).

His power is our power, but our power is not his power in

the sense that we are indispensable for his work. Nevertheless he has seen fit to exercise his power through the process of the fellowship and, in some sense, only through that process. If I am going to get the power to do what I want to do in terms of active love, there is no way in which I can bypass the process. In that sense the old church dogma, "Extra ecclesiam nulla salus" (outside the church no salvation), is right. Outside the fellowship of Christ's body, however painful and even boring at times, there is the power neither to be nor to bless.

EXPERIENTIAL EXERCISES

Exercise 1. Ask the members of the group to write down on paper as many synonyms for *power* as they can think of in five minutes. At the end of five minutes go back over the list that has been written and put a minus sign next to those words that have a negative connotation, a plus sign next to those that have a positive connotation, and a zero next to the words to which you personally attribute no value, positive or negative. Which category predominates in your list of synonyms? Discuss your feelings about power —not power itself, but your feelings about it. Are they generally positive or negative?

Exercise 2. Take a few minutes for the group to identify some situation they would like changed or some problem they would like to seek solution for, either in the community or the church. In a seven-minute period, brainstorm as many possible approaches as you can to bring about the desired change. After these are listed, identify the kind of power needed in each strategy suggested for the change you are seeking. For example, petitioning for a change to a governmental body will need to bring the power of a voting constituency to bear on the problem.

Exercise 3. Imagine trying to persuade another person to do something for which he or she has some reluctance. Draw a line horizontally along the middle of a page. List persuasions that you might bring to bear, placing the least powerful persuasions at the left and moving toward the right where you would place the most powerful persuasions you can imagine. Discuss together the rankings of various items, such as moral pressure or physical force, to see the power valuing system that different individuals in the group operate under.

Exercise 4. List and discuss the episodes in the life of Jesus where

49

he used power. Discuss the attitude he seemed to have about his authority in teaching, his driving the money-changers from the temple, or the moral persuasion he used with those who called for the stoning of the woman taken in adultery. What insights about power and its Christian use can you gain from such a discussion?

3.
MONEY

The Trouble with Money

IS THERE anyone who doesn't have trouble with money? Whether we have much or little, most of us worry that we don't have more. But have we done much thinking about the meaning of what we already have?

For many of us money is the least discussed area of our lives, at least in public. Privately, it may cause considerable anguish. We know that it is at the heart of a surprising percentage of divorces. But publicly—in church, for instance—we rarely discuss it except when we ask for contributions. "Money is the new pornography," a pastor friend told me recently. "People say, 'Talk to me about anything, but don't ask me how much money I make.'" When was the last time you heard the *meaning* of money discussed in a sermon or study group?

Under the surface, feelings of uncertainty and guilt are widespread. Inflation and recession, unemployment or the fear of it, are enough to create anxiety. Guilt comes from other factors: the sense that we don't use our money as wisely as we could, the discomfort we feel at the inequities in our society or the news of poverty and hunger around the world.

How should we as Christians talk about money? Does Christian faith affect our money attitudes and values, the way we *live* and the way we *give?* Can we be helpful to each other in thinking through our priorities, in assessing the power money has over us, in breaking through to new freedom—either *from* money or *with* money? Perhaps by taking the lid off and airing our views—sharing our understanding of what the Bible says and our life experiences as well—we can provide a forum in which all of us can grow in an understanding and commitment.

The difficulty has been that money arouses strong feelings and raises many questions for which there don't seem to be any simple answers. Christians speak with several voices. That will be clear as you read. And it should reinforce a conviction that grows on me as I study the subject: there is no one economic lifestyle prescribed in the New Testament.

That statement will disappoint some of my friends and be disputed by them. They argue that the biblical position is the *renunciation* of wealth and either a shared, communal style of living or a deliberate choice to live at a bare subsistence level.

They point to the early church and its initial instinct to share material possessions (see Acts 2:43–47 and 4:32–35). There we read that "there was not a needy person among them." And again, "All who believed were together, and had all things in common; and they sold their possessions and goods and distributed them to all, as any had need." It is important, however, to note that the tense of the verbs is imperfect, implying that *as* needs arose, someone reached out to meet the need. All the Christians did not necessarily sell all their possessions. And whatever they did, they did voluntarily, not under the compulsion of an order. (If this were not true, the actions of Ananias and Sapphira, recorded in Acts 5:1–11, would not be understandable.)

No, we are not told in the New Testament precisely how to deal with our money. We are told that material things are both necessary and good. We are told that God cares about our material needs . . . that as we seek his kingdom, our needs will be met.

We are warned about the "deceitfulness of riches," the danger of falling in love with money and its acquisition. We are admonished to care for the poor, to strive for justice and fairness in all our dealings. We are asked to give, not a "tithe," but generously, liberally, as God has given to us. But we are not given a prescription.

Each of us has to work out his or her own economic lifestyle. If we are serious about our faith extending to our finances, we will search the Scriptures for principles to guide us, we will ask God's direction in prayer, and many of us will share our search with fellow believers in the Christian community. (I am part of a small group that last year shared our budgets and counseled with each other.)

My own personal questions about money reflect a larger issue that I often find myself confronted with. I call it the tension between self-fulfillment and self-denial. I believe God wants me to be all that I am capable of being—to develop my gifts, to enrich my experience, to enjoy the world around me. I am also called to self-denial and service. Jesus spoke the words quite plainly, "If any man would come after me, let him deny himself and take up his cross daily and follow me" (Luke 9:23). It is clear to me that self-denial is one of the components of self-fulfillment—that part of "finding myself" is in living for others. But how do I balance the interests? Is it not equally true that the more I get for myself, the more I will be able to give others?

The question often involves money. Right now, I am planning to spend a month this summer studying on the West Coast, and at considerable expense. Here in the mail, today and yesterday, came pleas for money to help with hunger overseas. How can I justify any expenditures on myself when I am so much better off already than millions of the world's citizens?

The problem is more than a personal one. It is now national. We Americans have been living for a long time at the expense of the rest of the world. Our growth-oriented economy has required that we import 60 percent of all raw materials from overseas. Those resources are now dwindling, and the producer nations are demanding their fair share, as the Arab nations have been doing with oil prices.

We face a future many of us are not prepared for. The cost of living is probably never going to go back down to what we once enjoyed. Faced with increasing scarcities, we are going to be forced to live more simply. Our whole way of life in America may undergo drastic changes.

It's time to face this prospect, to anticipate it and ask what responsibility we have as a nation. Should we be sharing more with the world, or are we to put our own economic interests first? Each of us needs to face what his or her responsibility is.

A recent questionnaire in FAITH/AT/WORK made a start in this direction by asking some direct questions. From the heavy returns we are able to report the following conclusions which at least reflect the feelings of readers of the magazine.

Where do you feel most uncomfortable in discussing money? we asked and got three kinds of answers. 1. "At church," many wrote, implying their dislike for pleas to give. 2. "At home," others said, indicating that differing attitudes and commitment separated them from their mates. 3. "Among those who have much less than we, or much more," reflecting how money or the lack of it builds walls between people.

Of the first 163 replies we received, 47 make less than $10,000 a year, 54 make between $10,000 and $15,000, 41 make between $15,000 and $25,000, and 21 make over $25,000. One of them, in the latter category, wrote quite candidly, "I feel a double bind because we make so much and spend so much and like our living standard, while I know so many are living on so little."

And another asked, "Can anyone read Jesus' words about money in the Gospel of Luke without feeling uncomfortable?"

What portion of your gross income do you give to meet the

needs of others? Tithing is an almost universal practice of those who answered our questionnaire. But one conclusion is surprising. Those who make over $25,000 a year do not find it easier to give. Expenditures and lifestyles apparently have a way of expanding with increasing income. Those who speak with joy of giving are more likely to make less than $15,000 annually.

Do you deliberately live on less than you can afford? The answers were an almost universal no, except for money set aside for emergencies and old age. Some occasional exceptions are worth noting: "I live economically—don't buy luxury foods, grow my own vegetables, wear second-hand clothes, drive an older car." . . . "We give first and go without to do it." . . . "We have no need to impress our peers. Adequate shelter does not need to be fabulously furnished."

And some candid admissions reached us: "Yes," one reader wrote, "and I wish I did it for Christian/spiritual reasons, but I don't; I'm just plain tight." . . . "No, but I'm working on it." . . . "I could live on less." . . . "No, but I wish I knew how." One theme that ran through many of the replies was the recognition that Americans live at the expense of others in the world and that we ought to cut back our expenditures and seek a simpler lifestyle.

Our final question, *"Should antimaterialism be a part of our witness as Christians?"* aroused strong feelings and drew a wide variety of answers. We got yeses and nos and maybes in abundance. Here are some of the representative responses:

Yes. "Absolutely! Mammon is the number one American idol." . . . "Definitely. This is the subtlest and most malignant of the sins confronting us. I don't even realize it most of the time." . . . "Yes, yes, yes. By living more simply." . . . "Yes, our lifestyle should express it—not negatively, but joyously. This doesn't mean leaving beauty or pleasure out of our lives, but finding creative, even unconventional and not necessarily expensive ways to decorate our homes, etc." . . . "Christians are to be pacesetters in the art of sharing equipment: garden tractors, cars, washers—anything possible." . . . "It's best to travel light. Things are for us to use. They shouldn't control us in our decision-making, and we should be prepared to leave them or share them." . . . "We could live on 60 to 80 percent of what we make and give the rest away to help others less fortunate." . . . "We should hold our possessions lightly and not allow them to possess us." . . . "Pass the word that stewardship of what is entrusted to us is our response-ability to Him who gives it. He will stretch our dollars to cover both necessities and luxuries so that all we buy is a good investment." . . . "Yes, by living in community—putting everything in a pot to help those who really need help—that's how I'd like to live." . . . "Yes, by imagining and implementing alternative forms of economic and social relationships which do not depend so heavily on overconsumption of material resources."

No. "No way! Our Lord wants us to prosper." . . . "Our world loves money, so I think a wealthy person can have a tremendous testimony through his finances." . . . "No. Our witness is to Jesus Christ himself, a positive witness to a person." . . . "If a person has grown within, he'll more than likely take care of these matters without being preached to. I'd prefer to concentrate on the growth of a person, not materialism." . . . "I never liked the 'anti' approach. I would rather witness to the abundant supply of God's world and give thanks for the material supply as an added gift of God. Proper stewardship assures a flow of goods as a result not a goal." . . . "Abundant living does not exclude material things." . . . "Living in the midst of the material is important to me—living as the Lord's person in a world full of material of all kinds." . . . "Materialism is part of our gift of abundance and we can witness by our stewardship of the material things God gives us. My philosophy is: 'If I have it, God gave it; if you need it, please use it.'" . . . "No, no, no, no, no! What would we do without those dedicated people who gave to get this country going, with its churches, educational and other institutions, without those who taught giving, sharing, loving by setting their examples? Money is the means for doing much of what needs to be done. We have never found a way to do without it."

Maybe. "The term *materialism* disturbs me. It implies sackcloth and ashes. We should keep from worshiping the god of materialism by giving the tithe in creative ways and enjoy the other 90 percent as we use it to the glory of God." . . . "*Antimaterialism* is too strong a word. We all collect 'things.' We spend too much on material things and should spend more on having 'experiences' that feed our minds, like retreats, festivals, plays, workshops, musicals." . . . "The 'dangers of materialism' would be a better way of putting it. 'Antimaterialism' can lead to a 'spiritual' emphasis that is not biblical." . . . "I don't think if we work hard to earn our money it is wrong to enjoy it." . . . "I don't know. I know people who make a virtue of being poor, but they sure beg for money in their 'prayer letters.' Ugh!" . . . "I'm not sure. I don't know how literally to 'go and sell all you have.' Is it all right to dress well, have a large comfortable home and go on trips if I give 10 percent to help others?" . . . "We should be moderate in everything, not extremist. Both materialism and antimaterialism can be idols and divert us from our real usefulness for the Lord." . . . "I feel guilty, but helpless, in knowing how comfortable we are when so many are poor. I need a challenge and a guide as to how much and the best place to give."

If there was any consensus in all these answers, it was the affirmation that material things are not evil in themselves. What matters is how we use the money and material possessions we have. What are our priorities and goals?

The primary question, one respondent reminded me, is not "What shall I do with my money?" but "What shall I do with my life?" When that question is settled, guidelines for the use of my money will follow.

Perhaps the words of Proverbs 30:8–9, called to our attention by Dorothy Blazier of Knoxville, Tennessee, sum up best what our attitude ought to be toward money:

> Give me neither poverty, nor riches;
> feed me with the food that is needful for me,
> lest I be full, and deny thee,
> and say, "Who is the Lord?"
> or lest I be poor and steal,
> and profane the name of my God.

BREAKING THE POWER OF MONEY

John Levering

The first meanings of the Christian faith began to appear for me after I heard a sermon on money. I had been tagging along occasionally with my wife Dede when she went to The Church of The Saviour in Washington, D.C. Most of the sermons turned me cold. But this morning Gordon Cosby was talking about the meaning of money.

The church was launching an effort called FLOC (For Love Of Children) in which they were proposing to place in foster homes those of the city's unwanted children who then crowded Junior Village. It was a money-raising effort but Gordon came at the whole thing from a direction I had never encountered before. He talked about FLOC and what it was going to do, but the part I heard was about giving money itself—what the dynamics of that might mean to me.

That was a Sunday, and by Monday it was clear to me that I wanted to sell some investments and give the money. It wasn't so much concern for the project because I didn't have that much identification with the church or with humanitarian causes. It was an adventure in giving just for the sake of giving.

That was a totally new experience. As I look back on it, I can see that it started a chain reaction. It was the first step in breaking down a lot of old values—in this case, the way one uses money and property. It wasn't the first time I'd given something to somebody, but the only giving I'd ever heard of was people giving out of their excess, from pocket change, or at most, out of their income.

To sell investments in order to give money away was an

John Levering is an artist who lives in Columbia, Maryland.

"invasion of principal," a drastic break with the view of money as security. I didn't know anybody at all, in my family or at work or among my friends, who seemed likely to do such a thing. The prevailing view of life was that the world is a cruel place and will try to take your money away from you, so you need to squirrel away a nest egg and protect it carefully.

The sequel for me was important. Gordon Cosby's response was not so much a thank you for the sum of money as it was a celebration of my act of giving—an affirmation of my having done it.

That step became the entree into the church for me. Church and religion and, for that matter, even spiritual questions, just hadn't been a part of my life. I felt that if the church would leave me alone, I would leave it alone. We had a kind of detente. But now I started attending classes at The Church of The Saviour. It was the first exposure I had ever had to people talking seriously about what it means to be a person. They wove it all in with theology, an understanding of God and creation and living.

Theology wasn't a compartment off to itself; it was totally wrapped up in one's understanding of oneself, of other people, of everything that is. There was magic in that for me because it shed light on who man is, why we were created, what our role is in the world, and what our relationship to God is to be.

All of it had to do with the creative power of love and the necessity for freedom, because love has no meaning except with freedom. Personal freedom has many parts. Freedom in relationship to one's money is one of them and basic to all the rest.

I don't think you can deal with personhood, at least in our culture, without dealing with money. Money is the medium of exchange. It is personal power because with it you can do things, you can acquire things, you can cause things to happen.

Money is protection. With it you can protect yourself from parts of the world you don't want to be exposed to.

Money is security, not only material security but status, self-esteem. It is pretty hard in America to feel O.K. as a person unless you are "successful" and that usually means economic success. You know the saying, "If you're so smart, why aren't you rich?" It's in our language, in our slogans, in everything. So I don't think you can really have personal freedom unless you're dealing with the issue of money.

There's no secret to it. You can't serve God and mammon. You can't have two masters. Money has the capacity to be one's master, and that's what we're dealing with. To the extent our possessions exert power over us, there is no room for any other master. To the extent money represents security, to that extent we will never find or place our security in anything else. To be free, to live freely, we have got to break the power of money in our lives. One way to do this is to give it away; to voluntarily give enough that one's lifestyle must change, that one feels less security. This is exercising a new kind of choice about money. We reverse the power of money over us; we claim a new freedom.

I don't think it's a question of how much money we've got. Jesus told the "rich young ruler" to sell what he had. He talked to a lot of other rich people and there's no suggestion that he told them that. But with the rich young ruler, he was saying, "For you, as I see it, your money is controlling your life and you've got to deal with it."

I know that was crucial for me. Until all this began for me, my life was controlled by money. It took the form of working toward promotion, promotion bringing status and power. The process is hardly completed for me. Strong vestiges of the old value system remain. Now and then I think to myself, *one of these days you'll have an emergency you haven't provided for, and you're going to feel like a damn fool.*

But some things have really changed. I've changed vocations, and we have less money. We still live comfortably but on a lot less than we used to. I really value this. I value continuing to face these issues. They are really never laid to rest; they keep reappearing in new forms. But having less brings real freedom.

One of the freedoms is the freedom to fail. It fits a theology which understands our limitations as people. We are finite. We can't know ultimately all we'd like to know. What we experience as failure is simply over against what has been our definition of success. What we thought to be failure really might not have been.

In all of this I have come to want to live fully. One's life experience is as incomplete if he has never experienced failure as if he has not experienced success. Failure is a normal and prevalent life experience. Looking at it this way has made it possible to risk, and I have specifically wanted the experience of risking. That's the flip side of the old security that is being replaced.

In doing what I am now doing, I am using gifts I've always wanted to use, and that brings a sense of satisfaction. I don't need money in the same way. We don't take vacations as we used to, or buy things as we used to. And in hindsight I see that those things were substitutes for a deeper kind of satisfaction.

There's just no way that this would have happened to me without being part of a community. Our struggle with security is as much for our self-image and sense of self-worth as for our existence. Community can support and affirm us in taking steps that go against conventional values. It's hard enough to do, but it's a whole lot easier when there are folks around you who see things similarly and say yes to your actions.

There's a line in the Bible that I have a hunch has done more damage than we'll ever be able to measure: "It is more blessed to give than to receive" (Acts 20:35).

If you understand that to mean that the giver is *privileged,* well and good. But I don't think it is generally understood that way. We take it to mean that the giver is more *meritorious* than the receiver.

A central issue in all of this is the issue of control. The giver is usually in control and so the question arises, "What does giving really mean?"

There is a kind of giving that is giving away, giving without contingencies, with no strings attached, of saying to some of your money, "I'm going to get free of you." This demands a relinquishment not only of the money but also of control over how it is used.

This is a difficult area. Perhaps we need to distinguish between two kinds of giving. In one kind, to act responsibly, we need to make sure the money is used for the purpose for which we gave it. If we give to famine relief, we want to know it gets to the people and isn't pocketed by a government official.

There are times when giving with certain specifications is a very creative thing. And there are times when giving isn't appropriate at all.

But there's another kind of giving, giving in which we trust others in the use of the money. We don't say, "Play it my way or I'm going to take my bat and ball and go home."

I think one of the two or three absolutely central issues in what it means to be human is the issue of control. It is laid out in Genesis. In the Garden of Eden God and Adam and Eve are dealing with who is in control. God says, "I am in control," and Adam and Eve say, "We don't like the set up."

Control, power, security, God and mammon, personal freedom, faith, giving and receiving—such basic life issues! And at the core of each of them are questions about money. We are products of a money culture. It is where we live, and its vitality is something we have to face as we work through the questions of our own living.

Jesus represents a life of conventional value, turned upside down. One of these values, in our time, can be our understanding of giving—that giving is something one does for oneself. This kind of giving is not duty or grim burden; it is not paternalistic or manipulative. It is the only giving in which giver and receiver can be equal. This kind of giving is sharing and celebration.

CONFESSIONS OF A GREEDY CHRISTIAN

Bernie Johnson

I am thoroughly infected by our culture's values regarding money and material things. By nature I am a greedy man, and right now God seems to be making an assault on my conscience concerning this.

My condition is linked to "Johnson's first law of human motivation": *granted enough time, health and resources, I will end up doing pretty much what I want to do.* That can be freedom or vice depending on what I allow to influence my wants.

In my mind I tell myself that I could do without the material securities of my present lifestyle. "Just give me health, love of family and enough to eat, and I will trust the Lord forever." Nevertheless, I live in one of the better neighborhoods of our city. (But of course, that's only because the church I serve is there.) I make payments on a three-bedroom house (for the same reason). I operate two automobiles. (My work really calls for it.) I eat in restaurants several times a week (the work of ministry again).

I watch color television in a paneled family room. (The room came with the house, and we got a good deal on the TV.) I rent three telephones. (I wouldn't want to miss an important call.) I own two cassette tape recorders, two TV's, two adding machines, an automatic dishwasher, power lawnmower and a blow dryer. (You could hardly do my job and keep my commitments without these, now, could you?)

To be sure, I pledge money to my church and other charities.

Bernie Johnson is associate pastor of Westminster Presbyterian Church, Rockford, Illinois.

Frankly, it makes good tax sense. My motives are far from pure. I predict that unless there is a change in my actual values, I will continue to take care of myself first. I will "improve my lifestyle" with future salary increases, atoning a little bit by increasing my church pledge proportionately. This, together with thrift and frugality, has up until now accounted for my entire viewpoint toward money and economic responsibility.

I look around me and the economic imbalances in the world boggle my mind. Frankly, the social, economic and political factors that create the inequities are beyond my comprehension. Nevertheless, there is an inner voice that is saying to me, "You'd better struggle with this business of personal responsibility in a world rapidly reaching a polarization of haves and have-nots."

In this, as in so many other areas, I am still a "fraction," something less than a "whole number." But I have made some personal observations as I attempt to work this through.

First, much of my unnecessary spending can be linked to feelings of loneliness or failure. If I am temporarily discouraged, feeling like a failure, or just plain lonely, I will often go shopping or treat myself to something. I want to fill that emptiness somehow. Discernment is a subtle exercise, particularly when the budget can stand these unnecessary purchases. The fact remains, a new trinket or toy is often a symptom of my loneliness.

Second, I am defensive about my personal use of time and money. These are two areas that I want to control privately. It seems to me that most people are embarrassed about what they earn. They may feel it is either too little or too much. As far as time is concerned, what I do with my time outside of the hours I trade for wages is my business. I think these things are linked to my need to feel in control of my life. They are private domains. I am quick to justify every expenditure of time and money. I market a certain amount of my time which earns me the right to do exactly what I want with the time that's left over. My culture approves of this ethic.

But my confessed faith in Christ calls me to a new ethic. I can be freed from the life-stealing values of this world, so I am told. How can I do it, and what will it look like translated into behavior? The answer, for me, has to come in a small group or the trusted community of faith. I believe I will be on a new road as I begin to submit my time and my money to the scrutiny of at least one trusted brother. I am going to have to relinquish my private hold on these two areas.

I want a more radical lifestyle. I believe it calls for a more radical accountability. My guts flinch at the thought. I know the truth will call for change and that change will be liberating, but I am afraid—afraid I will not change at all.

The issue is not what I earn or how much time I have; it is what I choose to do with it. I want to be liberated to defy the culture's values in these areas. Let the culture pay me the going rate. Then let God and his people free me to a new way of distributing that time and money.

EXPERIENTIAL EXERCISES

Exercise 1. Take your bank statement and cancelled checks for the last month. Put the checks in five piles for these categories: (1) items related to our survival needs—food, housing, etc.; (2) items that are for us luxuries—things we enjoy but could do without; (3) items that involve our fulfillment of some kind of responsibility or duty—a payment to the United Fund, etc.; (4) pleasure items—things for which we can unashamedly say the purpose was pleasure; and (5) any expenditures that result from our intentionally living our discipleship to Jesus Christ. When you have completed the division into these categories, discuss the relative size of the money involved in each of them. How do you feel about the results?

Exercise 2. This is an imagination exercise in which you are to move around the group and answer quickly, without a great deal of reflection, "What would you order from a Sears Roebuck catalog if you had a windfall bonus to spend?" What would you get for yourself? What would you get for others? What might you get in response to God for living out your discipleship? What would you want to order for the world in which you live?

Exercise 3. This is a fantasy exercise. Imagine that the group in the room has been presented a check for $1,000. The group can spend it only if it agrees within thirty minutes on how it is to be spent. The limitation is that you must spend the entire $1,000 on one purchase. You need not be accountable to anyone outside the group for the choice that you make. Appoint someone to keep strict account of the time and stop after thirty minutes whether a decision has been reached or not. Next, talk about the assumptions about money the group made but did not state. Was fun or pleasure assumed to be good or bad? Was an effort made to benefit the whole group or to give it to some external cause that would not affect the group? Did some persons refuse to have a part in deciding? Was the use of money a "spiritual" decision?

Exercise 4. List the teachings about money that you can recall from childhood (family, Sunday school, etc.). Share these in the group. Which of these still influence your money decisions? How? Which have you updated? How and why?

Exercise 5. Read together the story of the rich young ruler in Mark 10:17–22. Allow some time for the entire group to identify with this young man. Let someone in the group take the role of the young man and defend his actions to the group in refusing to sell his goods. Now imagine another ending to the story. Imagine that the rich young ruler became a disciple and sold his goods. Let someone else in the group assume the role of the young ruler and explain his actions as if he were speaking to his own family. Following this, the group may want to discuss two questions: What problems in my life could be simplified if I had more money? and What problems in my life would be simplified if I had less money?

4.
LIFESTYLE

Living Together or Alone

WILL marriage, as we know it, survive?

A wide array of forces in our society today seems to threaten its traditional form if not its very existence. It seems, for many people, to be increasingly difficult to hold marriage together, and even more difficult to make it rich and rewarding. Among a growing number of married couples the search is underway for solutions. How is a Christian to find his way in changing times? Where does he look for guidelines?

Recently I was privileged to sit in on "A Colloquy on Marriage and Sex Values" held at Kirkridge Retreat Center in Pennsylvania, which brought together sociologists and clergypersons, men and women who are living in the traditional marriage pattern and some who are experimenting with new styles, to discuss these issues. I came away disturbed at much that I heard, but challenged to think through what our Christian faith may have to contribute. Let me report some of what I heard.

First of all, our present predicament was put in perspective. The institution of marriage, as we have known it, is obviously undergoing change. Divorce statistics were quoted and they aren't encouraging. The sex revolution is a fact. We're going to have to live with it. Issues are being raised that no one but a hermit can avoid.

At the turn of the century things were different. Society was based on a male-dominated hierarchy. Man was the bread-winner. A wife performed a domestic support role for her husband: she took care of the children, cooked and cleaned house, provided solace for her husband when he came home from work and a shelter of innocence in which the children could be reared. Families were larger than they are today. Grand-parents were often part of the household; aunts and uncles and cousins lived next door or up the street. The isolated nuclear family was rare.

Now all that is changed, not through some conspiracy to demolish our traditions, but through a historical process that resulted from innovations which we all welcomed at the time. Four factors have played crucial roles: the automobile, television, the pill, and economic prosperity.

Automobiles allowed us to be mobile, led us to build high-ways and escape to the suburbs. Increasingly men were able to live far from their work and were divorced more and more from their families. For teenagers, the automobile allowed privacy for sexual experimentation not permitted in their own homes, and was a major factor which led to relaxed morals.

Television has brought the world into our homes. The whole range of human experience—the sordid and destructive as well as the wholesome—has become commonplace to growing children. It is increasingly hard for a family to maintain values that go against the stream in a peer-oriented culture.

Contraceptives (and now relaxed abortion and sterilization laws) have separated sexual pleasure from the function of reproduction, raising radically new questions for sexual ethics.

And finally our affluence and leisure (at least for middle- and upper-class Americans) have made possible a whole new range of experimentation in attitudes and lifestyles, and insistent demands for self-fulfillment and personal satisfaction.

A "new woman" is entering marriage, or—in some cases—refusing to enter. Liberated by the pill, exerting her new-found independence to make her way in the world of work, and finding there are all kinds of new relationships with the opposite sex which were formerly reserved for men, women have changed the equation of marriage more decisively than any other factor.

At the same time marriage has been subjected to rising expectations. Something quite unique in history has surfaced in the modern Western world in the past centuries: marriage is seen as combining both friendship and genital sexuality. Andrew Greeley, in his new book, *Sexual Intimacy,* calls this "the real sex revolution."

The idea that a man should marry his friend and find not only sexual intimacy but emotional and intellectual companionship in one person is an ideal almost unknown hitherto in human history. But it is the ideal of modern Western society. And that's where the crunch comes. Marriage is asked to deliver the dreams of our romanticizing culture and is hard pressed to meet the ideal.

Is it realistic to believe that any single human being can meet all—or even most—of another person's needs? Should not a couple build a wider base of support by seeking additional relationships, be they intellectual, or artistic, or sexual or whatever—especially before pressures build up? Should they sublimate their unfulfilled energies by channeling them into other areas of interest? Or should they intensify their search for total satisfaction exclusively within the single pair-bond relationship? And is one style more Christian than another?

It does little good to make pronouncements. Simply to insist on monogamy or to preach against adultery and premarital sex is inadequate. We need help—all of us do—in thinking through the values we live by and learning to make our own responsible decisions.

We might begin by examining some of our present assumptions, whatever conclusions we reach as a result:

1. Is "exclusivity" and the nuclear family a Christian ideal? Perhaps the nuclear family (husband, wife and children living in isolated self-sufficiency) is more a product of our selfishness than any Christian motivation. The Christian impulse is to include people in community, to live openly in unselfish love toward others.

The church has always urged loving concern for the needy in the form of food and shelter, medical care and education. Have we neglected the emotional and social needs of those who may be lonely—whether married, single, widowed, or divorced? (Paul urged the early churches to extend such care. See 1 Tim. 5:3-7.) Perhaps we need to explore ways to enlarge our families to include people like this for our sakes as well as theirs.

2. What does fidelity in marriage mean? Andrew Greeley defines it as much more than simply avoiding the sex act with someone other than one's spouse. It covers a whole range of responses to one's partner which may ultimately be more significant than sexual fidelity.

The O'Neills in their best-selling book, *Open Marriage,* define fidelity as faithfulness to whatever contract partners may negotiate with each other. I heard much about this at the Colloquy. Many marriages suffer for want of a "clear contract" openly negotiated by equals.

We drift into marriage, repeating the vows prescribed by our church, assuming that there is only one form of the marriage contract, and that divinely given, without adequately sharing with each other our expectations. Only later do we discover that we have no common mind about money, about child-rearing, about the division of labor in a household, about a whole range of aspects in a demanding relationship. Or we grow in different directions within our marriages or at different rates, only to discover we are not the same people who originally covenanted to live together "until death do us part."

3. Is dissolution of the marriage bond always a sign of failure? Is it possible that it might be more constructive for some couples to divorce than to stay together? On this point the Bible seems quite inflexible. But churches, one after another, have had to find some way to adjust to the changing reality of our times. Perhaps our understanding of Jesus' teachings needs enlargement. Just as he put the needs of people before the institution of the Sabbath ("the Sabbath was made for man, not man for the Sabbath"), surely he would say that people should be put before the institution of marriage. Which ranks higher in a Christian hierarchy of values: people or institutions?

4. Finally, what should the church's role be in sex and marriage? I heard suggestions at the Colloquy that the church should relax its role (a suggestion also made by Martin Luther, we were reminded)—that it should advocate Christian values and leave individual Christians, within that framework of values, to work out their own patterns of sexual behavior. *But inwardly I wondered about such permissiveness. Do people not need to be protected against themselves with a framework of rules because of their propensity to sin? Is it realistic to believe that people left to themselves will make wise and responsible choices?* But more loudly I heard an insistence that Christians be allowed to grow beyond the need for external rules and learn to make their own responsible decisions—that this is perhaps part of the right given man as co-creator when God said to him, "Have dominion . . . and subdue" the earth (Gen. 1:28).

The discussion led constantly to an examination of the values we live by. At one point in the Colloquy the participants listed their values, distinguishing between those which relate specifically to sex and marriage, and those which transcend those categories and are basic to all of life. They not only found a surprising consensus among themselves, but when they compared the "operational values" to which their experience of living has led them and the traditional values of their Judeo-Christian heritage, there appeared a striking similarity.

They listed five transcendent values: (1) loving the other,

(2) accepting the other and granting him freedom and responsibility, (3) accepting the frailty and contingency of human beings, (4) maintaining open, honest relationships, and (5) affirming life—its enjoyment and adventure. *I wondered if the existence of God as author of the moral order was being overlooked or taken for granted.*

They listed six sex and marriage values: (1) Clear contracts or covenants, openly made by equals and periodically renegotiated, headed the list. (2) Continuing candor was seen as a necessary component of caring. (3) Fidelity was seen as reliability in keeping the contract and hence, a source of security within any relationship. (4) Accepting growth in oneself and others was seen as including whatever support or enablement of that growth might be in one's power to give. (5) A secure self-identity, including sexual identity, was seen as fundamental to establishing any healthy relationship with others. (6) At the last minute someone added, "a sense of humor," and it was agreed unanimously that that "pinch of salt" needed to be added to the stew. Healthy relationships require not only serious attention but "unserious relaxation"—the ability to not take oneself too seriously and to live happily within the givens of one's real world.

Reflecting for myself on these values, I came away with three disquieting questions. (1) Was the "fallenness" of human nature taken seriously enough? (2) Was sufficient recognition given to the fact (at least to me it is a fact) that we find life, in Jesus' words, by losing it? That we find ourselves by giving ourselves to something beyond ourselves? Again, in Jesus' words, that as we "seek . . . first the kingdom of God, and his righteousness . . . all these things shall be added unto" us? (3) Was the highest value, "loving the other," given a sufficiently active interpretation?

Is the quest to meet all my needs, to fulfill all my expectations, to realize completely my potential, ultimately self-defeat-

ing? Is happiness a by-product of the search for a goal outside of myself and beyond myself?

Some of us, as Christians, are just now learning to express our needs and wants and to realize that we have rights as well as responsibilities. None of us wants to give up this newly won territory. *But is there danger that in exercising our God-given freedom, the pendulum will swing—as it so often does—too far in the other direction? How do we hold together complementary goals and values: a proper concern for our personhood and loving concern for others? And what about society? Are there personal needs that should be temporized for the sake of preserving our larger cultural structure?*

Previous to the Colloquy a questionnaire went out to a thousand men and women who had participated in "occasions" at the retreat center. What were the most troubled areas in sex and marriage, they were asked. Their replies were selected from among premarital sex, pornography, abortion, how to revitalize dull marriages, alternate marital patterns, co-marital sex, strengthening sexual identity, divorce, homosexuality, and communal styles of living. Heading the list were: making divorce less hurtful and finding alternatives to traditional monogamy, including co-marital sexuality.

Divorce. The trend in our country is toward "no fault" divorce laws which makes "unmarrying" easier and will push divorce statistics up for at least another decade, with "snowballing" effect. But is the easier course always the better? Statistics show that few people learn by the experience of divorce. They tend to remarry the same kind of people they separated from. And divorce doesn't prove as liberating as it promised to be.

Opinion at the Colloquy was weighted toward the likelihood of large numbers exploring other styles of living rather than traditional monogamy, and of being more accepting of divorce. One person suggested that our laws be amended to raise the cost of a marriage license to $2500 and to lower the cost of divorce to $2, thus putting the stress on the need for adequate preparation for marriage. Some suggested that the church develop a ceremony to symbolize the death of a marriage (just as funerals symbolize the death of a person) and to allow grief to be experienced within the Christian community. Others suggested a new perspective: that the time may come in a marriage when its objectives have been achieved (childrearing, for example) and a couple may want to move away from each other. Why should this be thought of as "bad" if it allows the two to grow in new ways?

Alternate Marriage Styles. Some members of the Colloquy questioned whether we are *now* in fact a monogamous society. The premarital pattern of large numbers of college youth are radically different from their parents. The prevalence of cheating that goes on in existing marriages, and the advent of "swinging" styles of permissiveness suggests that promiscuity is rather generally accepted. On the other hand, statistics show that our society's verbal commitment to the ideal of lifelong monogamous marriage is still strong. The vast majority of young people look forward to it eventually, even if they are less sure of its meaning than they once were.

But monogamous marriage is in trouble and needs to be saved from both boredom, fragmentation, and unfulfillable expectations. One possibility is to explore co-marital relationships (as opposed to extramarital) in which facets of one's personality and needs not satisfied in the existing marriage can be fulfilled without threatening the marriage, but indeed being supportive to it. The distinction depends on whether such relationships are hidden from one's marriage partner or entered into with his or her full knowledge and approval.

The fear that any intimacy outside marriage will inevitably lead to the bedroom blocks many marriage partners from even beginning the quest. But why must intimacy lead that far? Are we not able to make our own choices? And need we fear enlarging our friendships if we have a firm sense of our own identity and a secure "pair bonding" with our mates? Do some of us lose a richness of relationships for lack of trust in our marriage partners?

In the final analysis our greatest fear may be not sex but intimacy. As one participant put it, "We are not so much afraid that our partner will go to bed with someone else as we are that she will come to love the other more and we will lose our priority."

Preparation for Marriage. One of the great concerns I took to the Colloquy and which the occasion did little to resolve is how to be helpful to children and young people growing up in today's society.

If marriage styles change radically to include easily accepted divorce, group marriage and communal living, what will happen to the children? Can children be adequately reared in group homes and communes? And is there any way to tell before it's too late to reverse the trend?

What is already happening to a generation growing up in an erotic culture, exposed to the "Playboy syndrome" of sex as recreation, supplied with the pill, and led to believe that "swinging" is as legitimate as marriage? There are voices crying in the wilderness that the Seventies will be the Age of Bisexuality. This is not to imply that all of us—if we just knew it—are equally divided in our desires toward heterosexuality and homosexuality—but that whatever one's predominant impulse may be (and we are being asked to accept homosexuality as normal behavior for some), we must recognize a trace of the other in ourselves and feel free to express it.

And how do we prepare young people for monogamous marriage fidelity if we still believe in it? Suggestions at the Colloquy included offering "encounter situations" where prospective marriage partners could make sure of knowing each other in greater depth. The Roman Catholic church was commended for its new Pre-Cana programs set up to meet this need.

Another suggestion was to be more sex-affirming in child-rearing: to be less prohibitive toward early sexual exploration, to model more sexual intimacy and touching in our homes so that children will be comfortable with sexuality and not see it as a forbidden, "naughty" area of life.

But how far should permissiveness go? What do we say to our young people when they ask what's wrong with previously frowned-on behavior? How do we respond when we learn for the first time that our son at college is rooming with his girlfriend?

These are the kinds of demanding questions we face in an age of unprecedented sexual revolution. And no one predicts that they are going to go away.

Can we handle the responsibility? Perhaps the greatest test of our faith will be to discover how it can enable us to make our own responsible moral decisions. And in the process we may find that rather than giving way on values that are important to us, we may be affirming them in greater depth.

THE JOURNEY ISN'T OVER

Wes Bryan

I will never forget the agony of sitting at the breakfast table with our five-year-old daughter. I asked her if she remembered about her little friend whose parents had separated and how his daddy didn't live with them anymore. She responded, "Yeah, but you'll never do that huh, Daddy?" And I had to answer with a hollow, "Yes, I'm going to, *now*."

I will never forget standing in the middle of that large living room piled high with boxes of stuff. Two piles as I remember, emotionally marked His and Hers like the bath towels we had received at our first shower some nine years before. The feelings of failure began to penetrate every area of my life. How often I had heard the phrase "alarming divorce rate." We talked, in this very living room, about other couples whose marriages were "in trouble." Now ours was. I couldn't help but wonder if we were doing "the right thing"—as if there were a single simple answer for all the complex feelings we were both having.

Some people had an answer for us: "Read this verse." "See this counselor." "Try that book." "Get in this group." It seemed to me that what underlined most of what many had to say was that if we'd just try harder, do more, somehow things would work out. And yet I had the strong sensation that things hadn't always worked out for them. But there I go, trying to defend, trying because so much around me still says so loudly: "You failed!"

That *failure* has touched every area of my life in ways I

Since he wrote, the author has remarried and uses the name Wes Bryan-MacLeod. He teaches speech communications at California State University, Long Beach, California.

never thought of: credit rating, job performance, social engagements, holidays. At every turn I was confronted with that harsh reminder that "I failed."

But even if in some way we could succeed in minimizing the socializing functions, there is the terror of the night, coming home to an empty house, cluttered and dim. The emptiness of that house spoke directly to the emptiness of my life, and at the times when I thought I was trying most to respond to Christ and his redemptive message. There seemed to be no redemption here. Lying in bed alone . . . how could I pray to a God up there . . . when I felt so cut off from human warmth and touch down here? For me those moments of intense loneliness were a living hell.

I began to consider the fact that there is no successful way to avoid these moments. They are not synonymous to divorce, they are synonymous to life. Divorce only forced me to recognize them in a particularly painful way. It seems that I have lived a million lifetimes running from loneliness, but no matter where I run—TV, books, projects, church activities, social events, groups, one of a hundred things which occupy time—suddenly I am keenly aware that I'm all alone.

The decision to separate did force me to acknowledge the pervasiveness of my aloneness. The aching nights which seemed to never end, clutching for the familiar shoulder only to find emptiness, getting off work to face a weekend which had previously been filled with family activities, panicked thoughts: "What will I do?" "Where will I go?" "How can I hide?" All of this seemed related to one basic issue: *What will I choose to do with my aloneness?* Most of my life I have chosen to run from it, refusing to acknowledge its existence or at least hoping to minimize it through activity.

Now as never before, it was focused with unusual intensity. At times I wondered if I would live through it. I think I would have given anything for it to go away, but it does not go away.

Clark Moustakas says it this way: "Loneliness is a condition of human life, an experience of being human which enables the individual to sustain, extend, and deepen his humanity. Man is ultimately and forever lonely." Even now that sentence causes a lump in my throat, because so much of how I have lived and am living has been a desperate attempt to quench that feeling. My relatedness to people, projects, and divinity have been with the inherent expectation that they would solve or at least minimize this condition.

That single expectation or demand has scattered the path of my life with unfulfilled promises, broken friendships, job dissatisfaction, heated arguments with God and now a broken marriage. All because I expected my loneliness to be answered. After all, the promise, "I will not leave you nor forsake you," was uttered by the very person who himself prayed, "My God, why hast thou forsaken me?" But, you see, it is at that very point I am beginning to see hope. It is not in the absence of loneliness that I identify most with Christ. It is in the profoundness of its presence, for both him and me.

It is at the depth of my own despair—when I am most inwardly convinced that I cannot make it—that hope and faith begin to quietly suggest that I will not die. And it is at that moment, maybe only at that moment, that faith makes any real sense to me.

Sometimes hope comes from deep within me, as if God were assuring me personally of my capabilities of withstanding this "habitation of dragons," as Keith Miller calls it. But this hope is not something which solves my loneliness, or makes for a victorious life. For me it is not acquired by believing a particular set of things, nor by performing a prescribed set of behaviors. Instead, hope seems to come with the very presence of a living God and brings with it the assurance that life has meaning.

From this position loneliness is still lonely, pain still pain, separation still separation, but there is a difference in the stance. Now I see hope not as a method of escaping these feelings, but as a means of living into them. I am beginning to grab onto life in a way that demands that I acknowledge the reality of my aloneness.

I can't yet put it all together, for me or you. At best I have merely described for you in some ways how things look to me now. Maybe they will be different for you, then again they may look very similar. Possibly it will encourage each of us to continue looking harder and longer because someone who is very much like you has continued the dialogue by saying, *Here is what it looks like over here. What do you see from over there?*

SINGLES FACE THE ISSUES

Paula Breen

There are approximately 49 million single people in the United States today. In the 1960s the adult single population jumped by two million a year. The estimation includes men and women who have never been married, widows and widowers, the divorced and legally separated. There are millions of single parents.

In an article in the February 17, 1974, *New York Times Magazine* ("49 Million Singles Can't All Be Right"), reporter Susan Jacoby notes that stereotypes about the unmarried "frequently seem as ludicrous as the image of a black population with a universal sense of rhythm and love for watermelon. Like any newly discovered minority, singles tend to be viewed by the majority in misleading, monolithic terms."

Who are these people and what do they have to say about being single? In an effort to find out more, FAITH/AT/WORK got together six men and women who are single for different reasons (widowed, divorced, separated, never-married, celibate) to discuss some of the issues they inevitably have had to deal with as singles.

Bill McCarthy voiced a strong objection to the stereotype of "single and lonely."

"They don't necessarily go together," he stated.

A divorced Catholic, Bill sees this period of his life not only as one where he can be open to new growth and change, but as one which gives him the opportunity to do battle with some of the negative forces working against him and other single

---

Paula Breen is assistant editor of FAITH/AT/WORK and lives in Columbia, Maryland.

parents. He has adopted what he calls a "Man of La Mancha" attitude, grabbing on to the challenge to use this time for good. "It's going to be good because I'm going to make it good."

One of his goals is to overcome what he feels is a judgmental stereotype in his church. "Divorcees aren't the nasty people one might think they are. There are a lot of wholesome, wonderful people who are trying to make the best of the situation in which they find themselves."

"That's why I became president of *Single Parents in Howard County*," he reflects. "I want to prove something to myself and other single parents: that we are not necessarily members in a 'Loser's Anonymous Club.'"

He sees his life as a ministry where, with the strength he gets from God, he can be a model and help other people through to true personhood.

Becoming a person who can stand alone was one of the principal goals stressed by everyone present. Sister Constance Fitzgerald put it this way: "I think there is really something in saying 'I'm me' without any apology." Having spent twenty-two years in a Carmelite monastery, Connie knows what she's talking about. The Carmelites have a hermit tradition which dates back as far as the twelfth century. "The life I live," she says, "forces one very soon to come face to face with oneself and to accept the fact that there's a solitude from which none of us can escape, no matter how deep our relationships turn out to be. To understand the basic solitude of the person is a real call in all of our lives."

Over the years, Connie has built deep and meaningful relationships with both men and women which would not have been possible, she contends, had she not first discovered what it is to be a solitary person. "The human person is really called to be at home in his own house, to find within himself the space to be. And many of us go through a long period of life without coming to terms with this reality."

Several members of the group claimed that weekdays after

work and weekends, when most families are together, are the most difficult times for them. Carrie Gardiner reflected, "Suddenly I was all by myself and whatever was going to happen was entirely up to me. That was aloneness."

Aloneness was seen as something different than loneliness. Loneliness, it was felt, is not necessarily resolved by marriage. As Bill McCarthy put it, "Loneliness is something much deeper —perhaps the absence of a spiritual tie with people."

Carrie agreed, "You can be very lonely in a marriage with somebody else sitting right there."

Loneliness, then, was seen as a fact of life for both singles and married people. Connie Fitzgerald pointed out, "We all know the terrible conflicts of meaninglessness in our lives. And there are many married people who are terribly lonely."

As with any group of persons outside the "norm," single people do not need to be patronized. Acceptance could very well be the name of the game for all of us—married or single. As one person put it, "I am what I am. Do you have the capability of accepting me for what I am?"

Perhaps the real question is, "Do I have the capability of accepting myself for what I am?"

Connie Fitzgerald said it well: "As single people, we've had the chance to deal with that question."

EXPERIENTIAL EXERCISES

Exercise 1. There are obvious pleasures and benefits from being with other people. Ask the group to name as many of these as they can in from seven to ten minutes. List these on a blackboard or newsprint. Give each member of the group a card with the instruction to list in rank order, one through ten, the most important of the benefits of relationships. After everyone has done this, group into fours and discuss the ranking each person gave and why.

Exercise 2. From the list constructed in Exercise 1, have persons individually mark down in three columns how they would rate each of the items listed. Column #1 would be labeled, "Only in Marriage," Column #2 would be "In Marriage and with Others," and Column #3 would be "Best Satisfied with Others." Share together in smaller groups where these have been placed and what they indicate about the nature of being single or married.

Exercise 3. For married couples: Individuals will be given time to develop a list of "The Richest Rewards in our Relationship." After the list has been written, hold a conversation with one other person who is not your partner to help clarify the meaning of each of these rewards. After the conversation, each person will write a letter to his or her partner expressing appreciation for the "Richest Rewards I Have Discovered." Partners should arrange a time during the following week when they can read each other's letter and discuss them together.

5.
THE BODY

At Home in our Bodies

BIBLICAL faith makes much of the material world, of which our bodies are a part. And yet the body is a subject often neglected among Christians. The initial declaration of Genesis about human beings tells us that God created us in his image, from the "dust of the ground," breathing into us the breath of life and declaring us, with all his creation, to be "very good."

The central truth of the New Testament is that God came in a human body. "The Word was made flesh and dwelt among us," we are told in John 1:14. We believe that Jesus Christ was God incarnate.

So important is the body in biblical faith that the Christian's hope for life after death lies not in a belief in the immortality of the soul but in "the resurrection of the body" (see 1 Cor. 15).

No wonder Archbishop William Temple once declared, "One ground for the hope of Christianity that it may make good its claim to be the true faith lies in the fact that it is the most avowedly materialist of all the great religions. It affords an expectation that it may be able to control the material precisely because it does not ignore or deny it."

Many of the great religions downgrade the body. This is

true of the wave of Eastern thought (Zen Buddhism, transcendental meditation, yoga, etc.) now washing the shores of our country in an unprecedented way. The concern of these systems in disciplining the body is in order to transcend it and produce a spiritual state detached from bodily desires, a "spirituality," we might note, that is unrelated to Christian faith.

Let me cite evidence. John D. Yohannon, in his *Treasury of Asian Literature* (The John Day Co., 1956), describes "the great truths of Buddhism (announced by Siddharta Gautama): that life is sorrow, that the cause of sorrow is desire, that escape is through the destruction of desire. . . ."

To many, the body—and the mind as well—is seen as a prison. Release is the goal of life. The mind's chattering must be stilled through disciplines of meditation. The body's desires must be overcome in the quest for peace.

This seems a far cry from the message of Jesus who said, "I came that you might have life and have it abundantly" (John 10:10), and who came not as an ascetic, like John the Baptist, but "eating and drinking" (see Matt. 11:18–20). True, he withdrew periodically to reflect and pray, and I'm sure he kept his body disciplined. But he also enjoyed it. He went to parties. He was very much "in the world," and lived an earthy life very much in his body.

Let us admit that such a biblical perspective has not always prevailed in Christendom. Too often Christians have fallen prey to the philosophy that informs Greek thought as well as Eastern, that matter is the source of evil. Much Christian history has been colored by an anti-body antisex bias, which is really un-Christian. The body is not the source of evil. That roots much more deeply in human nature. The body is neutral, capable of great good as well as evil, depending on what we do with it.

So, it's time we deal with the body. And there are three aspects we should pay attention to:

Accepting our bodies. Our bodies are an embarrassment to

most of us. They are either too fat or too thin, too tall or too short. They have defects we do all we can to hide. We certainly wouldn't want to be seen naked. Is comfortable acceptance of our bodies really possible? Does Christian faith have anything to do with it?

Being good to our bodies. How many of us take as good care as we can, or know we should, of the "houses we live in"? All of us, no doubt, could benefit from greater awareness of what our bodies need in the way of food, exercise, rest and attention, though most of us already know more than we are living up to. And why is it that we don't do better by our bodies? What does Christian faith say to us at this point?

Listening to our bodies. It comes as new learning to many of us to discover that the body speaks its own language, that what we think and feel and do is mirrored in our bodies and that our bodies respond with an integrity we contradict at a great cost to our physical, emotional, and spiritual health.

Wholeness demands that we get back in touch with our bodies and learn what they are trying to say to us so that we can grow toward a harmony of body, soul, and spirit. Biblical faith sees them as inseparable, so much so that the Hebrew language, in which the Old Testament was written, didn't even have a distinct word for *body*. As D. R. G. Owen, in his book *Body and Soul* (Westminster Press, 1956), says, "They did not need one, because they did not separate the body from the soul."

Let's not settle for either/ors when both/ands are called for, and this is surely one of those areas. In history and in culture the pendulum swings from one extreme to another. Our Puritan culture, compounded by Victorian attitudes, disowned the body. In reaction, some in the counterculture have swung to the opposite extreme with a wave of hedonism. And all of us have lived under the pervasive influence of Sigmund Freud who found so much repression of sex among his patients that the psychology he developed seems to proclaim sexual liberation as the bearer of health and happiness.

How can we avoid extremes and find constructive middle ground? How do we accept our bodies, how do we liberate them from repression, how do we come to live comfortably and in harmony with their rightful needs so as to integrate them, along with our emotions, our minds, and our spirits, into whole healthy beings? What Carl Braaten, Louise Cummings, and Nell Martin have written should give each of us added insight.

TAKING OUR BODIES SERIOUSLY

Carl E. Braaten

There has never been a Christian theology that takes the body seriously enough. We are only at the beginning of rediscovering a dimension of interest in the human body from the perspective of the Bible and the Christian faith.

Many factors have played a part in this process of heightening body consciousness. The ecology movement deals with the external environment of the body, arousing in us the desire for clean air and water. The natural food movement focuses on the interior ecology of the body, demanding real food good for the body. The peace movement has made us aware of the cold, dehumanizing references to murdered people in terms of "body count." The women's liberation movement speaks to the right of women to have control over their own bodies.

A favorite theme in Lutheran theology is the "whole person." Have we really meant it? Does it include the body, food, and the earth? The human body becomes concretely united with the earth through the food it eats. The whole person has a right to whole food from the whole earth. Instead, the earth is being plundered and polluted, food is being processed and poisoned, and humans are becoming more nervous and diseased. Living longer, we are enjoying it less. The quantity of life is growing by leaps and bounds; the quality of life is going downhill.

A theology of the body must be especially concerned about the earth and the food it yields, because the message of salvation comes to us in a sacrament of the flesh (Jesus), in a sacra-

Carl Braaten is professor of systematic theology at Lutheran School of Theology, Chicago, Illinois.

ment of water (baptism), in a sacrament of food (bread), in a sacrament of drink (wine), and in a sacrament of other bodies (the fellowship of believers). Christianity builds its whole message around the body as that is linked to the earth and the food it yields. Therefore, it ought to trigger an ethic of the body, that concerns itself for what capitalism is doing to our food to get rich quick at the expense of our health, how big business is destroying our earthly home to fatten itself at the risk of our future, and how the healing professions are treating symptoms of illness with expensive miracle medicines, neglecting the care of the total human person.

Increasingly doctors are dealing with degenerative diseases—heart disease, arthritis, diabetes, asthma, varicose veins, anemia, migraines, ulcers—which are not the problem at all. They are better viewed as the advance scouts telling us and our doctors —if only we had ears to hear—that we are not living right, we are not eating right, we are not thinking right. And we are asking technology to answer a basically theological question about the role of the body in life and salvation. We need a medicine of the whole person, but that is impossible when the pieces of the person fall into the hands of pure specialists, and religion, which should wrestle with the meaning of the whole, sits in its corner muttering something about higher spiritual values and the salvation of souls.

The first task of a Christian theology of the body is to undo the damage that Greek mythology did to biblical personalism. The Orphic myth taught that man is essentially a soul that has fallen into a body and is trapped there. The soul is the real self, the body is its prison-house and the purpose of religion is to liberate the soul from its earthly trappings, to help it ascend to its original divine home. That myth slipped into Christian doctrine and worked to reverse the incarnational current that God set in motion in becoming human flesh and blood in the person of Jesus. What we have to do now is to reverse the reversal, to get the incarnational current moving forward again with our bodies together with the earth as the God-given sources of their life.

The second task is to learn to accept our bodies as ourselves, to love them and become truly friendly with them. There's a French saying, "to fit neatly into one's skin." The body is created by God; it is good and grace-full. Surely, then, it is a disgrace to do anything to the body to disfigure it, to numb it, to flee from it, to hold it in contempt or silence it. The Puritan who trembles with fear when his body tingles with pleasure is a disgrace to his Creator; the saint who wants to please God by sacrificing one of his members has missed the message that God is sending through his body.

Brokendown Christians. It is always distressing to see "pooped-out" pastors and other brokendown Christians dragging along in their devoted ruins, making strong claims about their spiritual service to God and their fellowmen. Many of them are overweight and undernourished, out of breath and out of shape. Words about salvation come pouring out of their mouths, but their bodies are sacraments of damnation. Take a simple thing like breathing, for instance. One can't live long without it. Yet people attack it as though they hated their own bodies, by the foul air they breathe, by all the cigarettes they smoke, and by neglecting to get proper exercise and good nourishment for the organs involved.

Our third task is to appreciate the mystery of our own incarnation as the locus of God's redemption of the world. When God finally decided to redeem the world, he did not become a plant or a crocodile; he became a human being, a body-being, really some-body. God became a human person in Jesus of Nazareth. I don't know if he looked like our picture of him, but I believe he had a beautiful sun-tanned body in which he summed up all that God meant for our bodies to be. So, to be in the body of Christ is not to become alienated from our own bodies, but to come home to our bodies, and to yield them as the implements for doing the will of God (see Rom. 6:1–3).

Fourth, I make an ethical point. The attitude we take to our bodies is a sign of our attitude toward the world, the world of other people and the world of nature. If you despise your body, I am afraid to be near you. There is no telling what you will do to my body. Your body is you; if you cannot make the right choices with your body, you cannot be trusted in any way with my body. So I will try to leave you. You see, your body is the most eloquent message that you communicate to someone else. The most vicious Christian heresy is to separate spirit from body in such a way as to separate the gospel of salvation from the deeds of the body. What you do in your body is what you believe, no matter what kinds of words fall from your lips.

Fifth, the body is what keeps us down-to-earth, free from the heresy of "angelism." We are not going to become angels, no matter how hard we try. So why not settle for being human? We should become free from the idolatry of the body so abundant in the sexolatrous orientation of Western culture. To care for our body is not to worship it. Body care is one thing; body cult quite another. But in America, either we hate our bodies, showing contempt for the goodness of God's creation, or we worship them, bowing down to the body as a sex-inflated object. God's body, then, becomes a foreign body, something outside the integrated self, to be a plaything for oneself or others. Nothing is more sick in present American culture than the reduction of the body to the lordship of sex. Sex can thrive in a healthy body. When it becomes segregated as an object in itself, it becomes sick.

Inside the Body. Sixth, the human person is not only his body. That would be a reductionism. The person is potentially a spiritual body. Christians are not sheer materialists. There is the transcendent dimension of the spirit in, with, and under the body. I am my body, but not only my body. The body is both a component and a condition of my real existence. I cannot throw it away and live in a spiritually weightless state. On the other hand, there is more to me than my visible body. There is the inside of the body, the spiritual dimension. This is the body in ecstasy. This is the body going beyond its own limits, entering into communion with others in the power of love and the Spirit. When my body becomes open and harmoniously present to others, it is a sign that the Spirit of Christ is alive and effective. We find ourselves delivered from our individualism when we become persons in the communion of the body of Christ.

Here we reach a point of contact with the rich body-symbolism in the letters of St. Paul. Paul speaks symbolically about "this body of sin and death," the body of Christ on the cross, the church as "the body of Christ," Christ's body in the eucharistic bread, the resurrection of the body, the spiritual and glorified body, etc. But how do we read such body symbolism? I am afraid it usually takes off into the woolly realm of unclear and uncertain spiritual ideas, never to make contact with our material and mundane bodies again.

I am saying that a theology of the body never leaves the body behind. The very transcendence of God is not outside the human body of Jesus. Our Lutheran fathers were right in teaching that the one who is "very God of very God" himself is not outside the enfleshed humanity of Jesus. The movement of God's transcendence is incarnational. We always run the danger of letting God's transcendence hover vaguely outside our bodies in the holy smoke of some idealism or spiritualism. That is false transcendence, because it loses the center of gravity in the down-to-earth body of Jesus and his relationship to us. It is not elsewhere than in our bodies that we do our spiritual thing, whatever that is.

I believe Christianity is called today to preach the dignity of the body and to fight for its health on every front. We have preached long and hard against the lusts of the flesh, and that is right. Now we must attack the lusts of the spirit which lead us beyond the body into some "elsewhere." Nothing that bears on the health of the body of mankind is too trivial for Christian concern. We come from the earth and we return to the earth. Meanwhile, we exist as bodies. We need the food of the earth, or we become no-bodies.

MY BODY AND ME

Louise Cummings

There was a time when my body and I were inseparable. You could not have told us apart. When I was sad, my body cried. When I was playful, my body skipped around the block with hair flying, stood on its head, never minding what happened to my dress, or rolled in the fall leaves and dug tunnels in the heavy winter snow. When I was angry, it was natural for my body to join me in combat.

My body and I were loving with friends as well with the baby chicks, ducks, puppies and dolls I caressed and cared for. I was proud of my body. We won in stilt contests around the block. We shinnied up poles as fast as anyone and faster than most. We never lost our balance in crossing the top poles of swings. We climbed trees easily and they afforded us hour upon hour of fun. My body and I worked well together. I remember jacks contests and endless jumps of the jump rope. My body and I and life were all the same!

Then came adolescence. Sexual feelings were surprising and exciting at first. What fun to walk hand in hand with a boy and kiss! It felt exciting and fun until I felt the dark disapproval of my mother, looks that I took to mean I was a bad person. Then the words, "You're not weak; you don't need to hold on to a boy in order to walk." I knew it was the touching that she thought wrong. I soon computed it to mean that not only touching but all sexual feelings were wrong.

As soon as I found out certain feelings were "wrong," their intensity increased and they raged and roared within. I told my body, "We must never let on; we won't let the world see

---

Louise Cummings is a pseudonym for a homemaker who wishes to keep her identity unknown.

what's happening inside." That started a separation between me and my body that lasted for years. I remember a talk given in church about a girl's responsibility as far as clothes and mannerisms are concerned, and from that I concluded that I was responsible not to stir up boys' sexual feelings. If a boy felt attracted to me, it was because I was doing something wrong. I started wearing sweaters loose enough to conceal any development that might be happening underneath, to walk with hips hardly moving, to sit with legs all but glued together, and to laugh with my mouth closed and my body still.

Through most of my twenties my heart was big enough to care for people but my arms hung at my side. Even after marriage I was hesitant to caress my husband unless I was sure we were alone, and then there often was no *real* freedom. Only my babies allowed me the freedom of caressing, loving, and freely touching. My spirit was "jumping and leaping and praising God" but my body only tapped its toe. I longed once again to run free with the wind and be spontaneous in movement. I felt weighed down with the responsibility of controlling this uncontrollable body.

My body and I stayed unrelated until problems with colitis forced me to take a look at our relatedness. The first time colitis forced me on a strict diet and limited activity was when our second baby was born within thirteen months of our first, and my father was having exploratory brain surgery. The second time was during a worrisome period when our son was sick with an unnamed digestive disorder. Here were *other* things I couldn't control and my unexpressed fear, stuffed deep down into my bowels, evidently reacted in my body to form colitis. Only now am I beginning to learn to recognize fear and call it by name before I slip a control on it and deny its presence.

Since the days of colitis I have taken many steps forward as I have sought to become reunited with my body and my feelings. The first was touching a young boy's arm in tenderness, when I was thirty, as he stood at our door asking forgiveness. The next was a momentous release from false guilt over a sexual incident through a memory healing prayer, following which my physical life with my husband took on whole new joy. Another step was using the gift of a week at a Faith at Work Leadership Training Institute several years ago, letting my body, though awkward at first, act out my feelings of praise in response to music. After that I did some rather intensive releasing of feelings at a "Shalom Retreat" at a retreat center, Kirkridge. For many years feelings had gone unacknowledged. Is it any wonder that it is taking many steps to become reunited?

I like to hug and touch people I care for. I love to be hugged and touched by them. At one step along the way, out of fear of activating the giant sexual feelings within, I limited my male hugs to my husband, my father, and my boys. What if I were to feel that surge of excitement while hugging someone other than my husband? Then I dared. It was when I risked hugging other men who meant a lot to me that I began to find the giant diminishing in size and no longer being a problem.

Had I been misled all these years? Where has the uncontrollable giant gone? Is it possible that a hug can be complete in the joy of a hug? That touch is to be enjoyed as touch? The intimacy I now feel in a hug can be savored legitimately for just what it is. It does not need to lead to something else without which it is unfulfilling.

Lately I've been intrigued by the accounts of Jesus touching those about him. I'm aware that his touch was highly valued as a means of healing by the people who gathered around him. There is an account of friends begging Jesus to touch a blind man. Through touch Jesus healed a leper. He wanted the children to come to him so he could touch them. And he did not shrink from the touch of a woman.

Feelings have become my friends at last—to be rejoiced in for themselves. They remind me of my aliveness, of my real love for life, and my gratitude that once again my body and I are one. Why, when you look at my body now, you can almost always see me!

I ENJOY BEING A WOMAN

Nell Martin

Six years ago I "found myself" at a Faith at Work conference in Germantown, Tennessee. I was a brand new baby Christian—full of enthusiasm, love, joy, peace and all the other good feelings you can think of. When I said, "God, you manage me. You take over. I want you to be the director and I'll just follow your directions," I felt his "anyhow" kind of love pour into me. I knew that I had truly found myself. Little did I realize that I was just beginning my search.

In these last few years God has shown me area after area in my life where old illusions, old attitudes, old prejudices needed to be shed, reevaluated and clarified. One of the most recent has been in the area of my own sexuality.

I was brought up in a conservative religious family in a southern city. I graduated from a very small exclusive girls school, in a culture where nice girls just didn't "do it." (I couldn't even say "sexual intercourse" at the time.)

All I knew about sex was that I had very good, tingly feelings for some of the boys I dated, but that to do anything with them other than just kiss, was *bad*. Whenever I did go beyond the good night kiss, I felt guilty. Already, at sixteen, or seventeen, that adjective was attached to all sexual feelings.

I graduated from high school with my virginity and went off to college. The first Saturday night of my freshman year I walked down the steps of a fraternity house and there he was—"Mr. It"—my lifelong dream. Bells rang, my blood raced, and my heart pounded. Bill Martin didn't have a chance. I knew what I wanted and he was it. Two years later

Nell Martin is a homemaker in Sheffield, Alabama.

we were married—with the white dress, all the trimmings, and my virginity all very properly intact. Whew! I had made it. I was a "good" girl. I had avoided the pitfalls and now I was safely married.

For twenty years I had felt that nice girls didn't and now I could, because I was married. But when I did, way down deep inside of me I still felt bad, guilty and very shy. I didn't tell Bill about my feelings at the time because I was afraid he would somehow personalize them and feel that I didn't love him. I didn't talk about my feelings to any of my friends because I was ashamed of them. I just assumed that no one else felt as I did. They were all O.K., but I wasn't.

Bill and I have been married twenty-one years now and the last year has been the most fun, the most free, the most exciting year in terms of my sexuality.

One of the things that has really been helpful to me has been the new books I've read on sex: *The Sensuous Woman, Human Sexual Response* by Masters and Johnson, *The Art of Loving* by Erich Fromm. I realized how much more there was to sexual intercourse than what I had allowed myself to feel. For most of my married life intercourse had been more of a duty than anything else. "A satisfied man at home doesn't have to look elsewhere." "Never say no to your husband." So to protect myself, my children, and my home, I did my duty many times when I was worn out, angry, hurt, or just plain bored and ended up with resentment toward Bill but ultimately toward myself. Something was really wrong with me because I didn't enjoy sex more.

I even made an appointment with a psychiatrist. He told me I was better off than 75 percent of the women he knew. It would take a lot of time to get at the root of my problem, he concluded, and when he had the time, he'd call me. That was the last I heard from him.

Bill and I made an appointment with a family physician and went together to talk about our problem. The doctor just confirmed what deep down I already knew: there was nothing wrong with Bill. I just had some deep psychological hang-ups which would probably take professional help to cure.

Praise the Lord I am married to a guy who is sure enough of his own sexuality not to let my attitudes about sex become personally directed toward him. If I'd been married to Rudolph Valentino or Clark Gable, I'd have had the same problem.

Through a friend we heard about a Human Sexuality Lab that was being held in a nearby community. It was being sponsored by a medical school for doctors so we felt reassured about the quality of the leadership. Both of us were scared to go. We had no idea what we would get into. But we made a contract with each other before we went that if either one of us wanted to leave at any time, we would.

Saturday morning the lab started with some of the usual get acquainted games, then a film called "Looking for Me" about four or five-year-olds discovering their own bodies and enjoying them. Gradually we worked up to a film on masturbation with a young teenage boy, then one with a young teenage girl. There was a film on homosexuals, both male and female, then four or five films on heterosexual relationships. These were beautifully done. The sound effects were of nature —the sound of the ocean, a field of flowers blowing in the wind. After each film we would break up into small groups (with husbands and wives separated) and share our reactions to the films.

People were open and honest about their "hang-ups" on sexuality. I was like a child turned loose at the midway with free tickets on all the rides. I asked all kinds of questions that for years I had wanted to ask. I was able to talk about feelings that for years I had been ashamed of. Forty-one years of curiosity was pretty well satisfied and I left that weekend appreciating my body—and Bill's body—as two of the most beautiful gifts God has given. Bill and I were able to talk freely about our feelings, our needs, and how we could give to each other in new and different ways that would be meaningful to both of us.

Not only have I seen a change in my relationship with Bill, but I have seen a change in my relationships with other men. I had assumed that intimacy with a person included sexual intercourse and so I had been afraid to allow myself to become too close to any man but Bill. Now I am more sure than ever that my value system excludes extramarital sexual intercourse, but it does not exclude close male friendships that I had deprived myself of all those years.

I had not committed adultery for a number of reasons, but one of the main reasons was that I was not free to. Not only did I not enjoy sex that much, but I would be *bad* if I did. Besides, I was sure I wouldn't *measure up*.

Now that I feel more acceptance of my own body, now that I have discovered more about intimacy and my own sexuality, I am more convinced than ever before that I can choose— not because I have to, or because God wouldn't love me if I didn't—to have intimate relationships with both males and females without sex. And I choose to have sexual intercourse only with my husband. It makes our relationship even more special because we have chosen each other to share this part of our sexuality with.

You know the old Broadway song, "I Enjoy Being a Girl." Well, I can shout it from the rooftops now. I really enjoy being a woman. God has neat gifts for each one of us—to meet our every need—and he has just recently given me a new one that I can enjoy until the day I die.

EXPERIENTIAL EXERCISES

Exercise 1. Frequently we have limited our perception of how our bodies are received or seen by others. In this exercise each member of the group will be given a number of slips of paper equal to the number of persons in the group. There will be an envelope bearing each person's name. As the envelopes are passed around the circle, each person will write down what he thinks about the physical appearance of the person whose name is on the envelope and put that slip of paper into the envelope and pass it to the next person for his/her impression. After the envelopes have made the full circle, they will come back to the person whose name appears on them. Then the group will divide into smaller groups of three, while each person opens his/her envelope, reads off the observations, one by one, and either affirms or questions each of the observations. Following this, the total group may want to discuss the observations that were made about them by others.

Exercise 2. Write down five things you were told about your body as a child. These may concern your birth, your strength, your dexterity, your size, or any other aspect of your physical body. After you have written these five, reflect on how you hear these messages now. Do you still respond to them, or have you discarded them? Discuss this with one other person in the group.

Exercise 3. Make a list of truths that you can affirm about your body. Which of these do you think Jesus could have affirmed about his body? What about your body could not have been true of Jesus? How do you understand the statement about Jesus, "the word became flesh" (John 1:14)?

Exercise 4. On a large sheet of blank paper draw a caricature of yourself using the following guidelines: Let the size of various portions of your body indicate the importance they carry for you and color each of them with a color that represents how you feel about

103

that part of your body. For example, if you have great respect for your brain, you might draw your head very large in relation to your shoulders and body. Share these drawings and explain them to others in the group.

Exercise 5. Sit in pairs facing each other with your hands touching. The following exercise will be done in complete silence with your eyes closed. Let one person be a receiver and the other a sender to communicate the following feelings: (1) anger, (2) care, (3) sorrow, (4) joy. Now reverse the sending and receiving roles without speaking, and repeat the four feeling words. Having done this, have a conversation about the experience. How skilled were you at sending touch messages? Could you understand the messages you got from the other person?

6.
PATRIOTISM

Being a Responsible American

AS WE think of our nation's 200 years of history, I wish all of us who are Americans could hold a great Town Meeting. Or at least that a few of us could pull up our chairs around an old-fashioned pot-bellied stove and talk. But before we shared our ideas—what we think is right about America, or wrong, and what ought to be done about it—perhaps we could begin by telling our stories. How have we actually experienced America? What freedoms do we enjoy? What limitations have we known? What do we wish we could have experienced?

I want to share some of the experiences that have shaped my feelings and attitudes. It doesn't seem fair to do so without hearing yours which are just as valid and important, but talking about my own story may prod you to recall your own and reflect on it.

My first memory of America was of coming home to it from a foreign country. I grew up in China, where my father had gone to teach, and have always felt that if it is a privilege to be an American, as I certainly believe it is, I have had a double privilege. I can see what it means to be American, but from a unique perspective. America is great, but the world is far larger than America. One of the benefits of travel is not only to see other countries but to come back to our own with broader perspective.

All of us, I suppose, tend to see our own country as the center around which all other lands are ranged. The Chinese certainly do. It is with justifiable pride that they look back to centuries of culture and their name for their country is, quite naturally, "Middle Kingdom."

There is a sense in which every land has, or needs to have, its own sense of pride. And a proper love for country doesn't have to lead to narrow provincialism. It can be the healthy basis for a universal love. Thus, I can love America but believe that it is no more important to God than any other country. "God so loved the world . . ."

A visiting speaker at our church recently, a Christian who works in government in Washington and knows his Bible well, was asked, "What is God's plan for America?" "God doesn't have a plan for America," he replied; "He has a plan for the world." I believe that.

Two memories stay with me from my college days in Illinois. Our college president used to quote Paul, from Romans 13, and bear down on the loyalty Christians owe their government, since all governments are "ordained of God." He took pride in recounting his war experiences, having fought "to save the world for democracy" in World War I. But at the same time he talked with pride about the old building downtown that had been a station in the Underground Railroad during the Civil War, a refuge for slaves fleeing north to Canada and freedom. I don't remember him trying to harmonize the loyalty to country that led him to bear arms in World War I with the loyalty that led the Abolitionists to defy unjust government in the days of slavery. But the lesson was obvious. Governments are necessary. One subjects himself to them. But if the two clash, the choice is clear. "We must obey God rather than men" (Acts 5:29).

I was young and idealistic then. Issues were always clear,

black and white. There were no ambiguities. A Christian always knew where to stand. And there would be glory days ahead. Somewhere, sometime, I would take my stand and be a hero.

I read the Book of Acts and saw how the early Christians came into conflict with government. In doing so they acknowledged the prior claim of God on their lives, asked him for courage to be true to the truth, and went on boldly proclaiming their faith in Christ.

I recalled my boyhood days in China and the special status we had by treaty with the Chinese government. We came under Chinese law and if we broke the law we could be tried and sentenced, but we were American citizens with an overriding loyalty to our own country. So the sense of living in the world but having my citizenship in heaven, as the Apostle Paul puts it, was reinforced vividly in experience. And it was only natural, when my consciousness was raised, during the Civil Rights movement of the 1960s, to the injustice that was being done to black people in our country, to assert my loyalty to justice and commit acts of "civil disobedience."

My most vivid memory of that time was of living with black people in a segregated southern town and, in marching with them for equal rights, to be followed everywhere by the police and the FBI (if I have correctly identified those who shadowed us) and sense something of how black people have for generations been deprived of their rights as citizens.

It felt good and right to put myself in danger for the cause of justice. I felt the presence of God with me. And something in me still feels that way. I long to see Christians take the lead in confronting the great moral and social issues of our time. I see people running after this experience and that, in order to gain a sense of power. If we are powerless, perhaps it is because we are too much turned in on ourselves and too little engaged in the search for justice in the world. When we wed moral and ethical power to the power of faith, we will be powerful indeed.

For a long time I have felt prejudice against southerners in our country. On the one hand, it is "the Bible belt," the region where church attendance and Christian commitment is highest. On the other hand it is the region where racial injustice has been most institutionalized. But in recent years I have come to feel that the South will reach a quicker and better resolution of this fundamental injustice in our society than any other region. When consciousness is raised, Christian faith empowers people to act compassionately.

But the moral issues in a society are not always seen clearly. We tend to dismiss them as "political" and say that discussion of them belongs outside the church. Or we are blinded to them by our own self-interest. We do not easily see that the system of which we are a part gives us privileges not granted to the poor. Our tax laws, for instance, may be shot through with injustice and inequality, but because we are the benefactors we are slow to see and admit it.

And there are many gray areas. The issues are seldom black and white. I was reminded recently in church of the need for discernment in facing the questions before us in our country. Our lesson was from Matthew 22:15–22, the story of Jesus' encounter with Pharisees and Herodians who were trying to trap him. "Is it lawful to pay taxes to Caesar?" they asked. Intellectually, at least, Jesus' questioners had their own simple answers to that question. "One must always obey God," the Pharisees said. "One must obey the government," the Herodians insisted. But Jesus confounded them. "Render therefore to Caesar the things that are Caesar's," he said, "and to God the things that are God's."

Jesus wasn't making a clever dodge. He was pointing to the ambiguity inherent in many decisions we have to make and the need for discernment in each individual case. The choices are not always clear and the followers of Jesus must learn to live with ambiguity.

But it seems to me that there are two principles we, as Christians, have to make up our minds about:

1. Are we to work only "within the system" to bring improvement, or will we challenge the system and seek to change it when we see injustice in it? There is a fundamental cleavage between Christians at this point. None of us questions the validity, or necessity, of acts of compassion and mercy. But to some this is merely Band-Aiding. If the system is wrong it needs to be changed. And it is hard for me to see how people who refuse to challenge unjust structures can at the same time glory in the American Revolution which declared its independence against social injustice.

Jesus told a story about a Good Samaritan who stopped and showed mercy to a man who had been robbed and beaten on the road to Jericho. Would it not make sense to provide protection along that road to insure safety to others who traveled that way? Are you willing to go beyond mercy to what one friend of mine calls "preventive social concern"?

2. Must Christian action be limited to individuals acting alone or can churches (either local churches or denominations) take concerted action to change the structures of society? No one, that I know of, questions the right of churches to perform acts of mercy—to operate rescue missions, schools, hospitals, etc.—but the moment concerted action is proposed to influence legislation that would alter social structures a hue and cry arises that "the church is getting into politics."

Perhaps to raise the issue is to answer it. Is there any question that is merely political? Do not all issues have a moral component? And is our conclusion on the matter not based, in actuality, on which issue we are talking about? We may approve the church's acting against pornography or for prayer in the public schools but not for fair housing or voting rights.

The questions demand hard, realistic answers. And Christians are not exempted from participation, especially in a democracy that gives us not only the privilege but the responsibility of speaking and acting on our convictions.

We are told, in Romans 13, to subject ourselves to government. We are also instructed, by the whole tone of Scripture

—Old and New Testaments—to assert our basic loyalty to God and to speak prophetically when we see evil and injustice going unchallenged.

We need discernment, and discernment is one of the gifts the Spirit wishes to give us. It does not come automatically to Jesus' followers. Read the Book of Acts and you will discover that Spirit-filled men and women were still racial bigots. It took time and many hard lessons for them to open their doors to Gentiles. And we have not fully learned the lessons yet.

As we enter our nation's third century, and as we Christians approach our third millenium, we still have a long way to go in understanding and living out the claims of our Lord Jesus Christ on our lives.

THE CHALLENGE OF THE BICENTENNIAL

Where is America going? What needs to change? How can Christians serve both God and Country? These were the issues that surfaced at a recent dialogue on "A Responsible Patriotism" held at Kirkridge in Pennsylvania's Pocono Mountains.

Kirkridge director, Robert A. Raines, invited the third ranking Republican in the House of Representatives, Congressman John Anderson from Illinois's 16th District, retiring Yale University Chaplain, William Sloane Coffin, Jr., and his brother John Raines, who is professor of Religion at Temple University, to an informal discussion of the issues and invited FAITH/AT/WORK to report what was said.

We have chosen to present the gist of two of the statements made at Kirkridge, one by Congressman Anderson, the other by William Sloane Coffin. We report what they said not as a statement of FAITH/AT/WORK policy but in order to stimulate and inform an ongoing discussion of the issues as we step into the third century of American history.

John Anderson's Statement: We are at a critical juncture in our nation's history, a period of difficult transition, searching for new direction. We are no longer so sure of ourselves or where we are going. We have seemingly lost our moral moorings and are a nation adrift on a sea of uncertainty and doubt.

The American revolution brought out both the best and the worst in Americans. Don McLeod, in an article in *The Washington Star,* amply documents this observation. He reminds us, "One of the lesser traits of the American character to emerge in the rebellion was a harsh intolerance of anything viewed as a threat. Loyalists were subject to the very abuses

111

which had driven the patriots to war—censorship of press, speech and action, unreasonable search and seizure, even troops billeted in their homes."

About a hundred thousand Americans, one out of every twenty-five, were forced to flee to Britain or Canada from the wrath of their fellow Americans. Those who stayed on paid a heavy price. Men, acting in the name of liberty, were accused of "chaining men together by the dozens, and driving them, like herds of cattle, into distant provinces, flinging them into loathsome jails, confiscating their estates, shooting them in swamps and woods as suspected Tories, hanging them after mock trials; and all this because they would not abjure their rightful sovereign and bear arms against him."

McLeod notes that "when the war was over, the United States adopted a Bill of Rights. It was too late to help the Tories, but it did guarantee most of the rights they had lost and secured future generations from such punishment for their beliefs."

So there has never been a time in our history when there existed pure and virtuous patriotism. Patriotism, or love of country, can be just as pernicious as it can be virtuous, and our history is replete with examples of both forms. One need only think back to our recent Watergate episode and the assault on our constitutional system by those wearing American flag lapel pins to confirm the truth of this observation.

Patriotism more often than not, however, manifests itself in a third form—a passive patriotism, unthinking, unquestioning and uncritical. And passive patriotism has potential for being aroused for either good or evil. But because it is unthinking, blind loyalty, the chances are great that it will be misdirected when it is aroused.

Just as personal love is sometimes blind, so too can love of country be blind. How many Americans, during our recent Vietnam upheaval, were heard to quote Stephen Decatur's "My country, right or wrong"? "America, love it or leave it," is an example of blind love. "America, improve it or lose it," is responsible, constructive patriotism.

In his famous work, *Democracy in America,* the Frenchman Alexis de Tocqueville defined a kind of patriotism that "springs from knowledge; it is nurtured by the laws; it grows by the exercise of civil rights; and in the end, it is confounded with the personal interests of the citizen. . . . A man comprehends the influence which the well-being of his country has upon his own; he is aware that the laws permit him to contribute to that prosperity, and he labors to promote it, first because it benefits him, and secondly because it is in part his own work."

A new form of patriotism may indeed be emerging, one that will be shaped by the new realities of finite resources, global interdependence, the diminished role of the individual in our technological age, and opportunities during a period of detente to project positive American values abroad.

In his article "Reshaping the American Dream" in the April 1975 issue of *Fortune,* Thomas Griffith contended, "Americans uneasily sense some permanent change in their condition, and see more change required of them, even if they are sometimes daunted by the lengthy agenda of what needs doing. In the doing of these things, however, there may yet return a pride in accomplishing them together. The merit of freedom, so instinctive to the American character, and not lightly to be surrendered, has always depended on the unforeseen uses that can be made of it. The direction that this nation is now taking is certainly not clear. . . . It may be that for a long time we will be unable to define the new kind of society we are making, but will simply discover ourselves living in it."

I would like to think that common consent over our national purpose will be more deliberate and purposeful than the revolutionary drift which Griffith foresees. If we simply allow ourselves to be swept along by events and forces beyond our control, there is little chance that we will have any control over our fate under the new society which evolves.

There is a real need, in this transition period, to rearticulate and reaffirm the common core values on which our nation was founded. As I assert in my book, *Vision and Betrayal in Amer-*

ica (Word, 1975), "Only a renewed commitment to the basic core values of democracy can save our pluralistic and diverse society from ruin. . . . Our problem is not that our national values have failed us. It is rather that we have failed them. We do not need new values so much as we need new commitment to the old ones. If we can renew our dedication to the noblest of the values in our constitutional tradition, we will be well on the road to recovery."

This, it seems to me, is the challenge to build a responsible patriotism in bicentennial America. It involves restoring a sense of community based on a sound system of traditional values. It involves a reawakening of all Americans to the linkage between their personal interests and the national interest and their obligation to actively pursue these on a sustained basis. It involves a new moral commitment on the part of leaders and led alike to a new national purpose and direction. And, finally, it involves a new willingness to communicate between diverse groups in reconciling differences in the pursuit of our national goals. If we can approach our third century in a spirit of responsible patriotism, I am convinced we can recover our lost confidence and go on to build a better America.

Bill Coffin's Statement: I have very positive feelings about where we are now in America. It's a great time to be patriotic and an even better time to be religious. We're going through a time of disillusionment. But who ever gave us the right to have illusions in the first place?

While we're a cradle of liberty, we're also the only nation in the history of the world that was founded on the blood of ten million Indians and developed on the sweat of forty million slaves. We can't get away from the consequences. The sins of the fathers are visited on the sons and their children unto the third generation.

We're losing our innocence as more and more truth comes to light. We ought to rejoice, because in passing from innocence the option of holiness is ours. The problem with truth, however, is the unacceptability of truth that is unpleasant, especially if you're brought up as an American.

It seems to me it's good that disillusionment is coming about. Though it's terribly difficult to lose one's illusions, we're coming into an age of honesty. But it is also a terribly dangerous moment because somebody could come along and try to recapture the pleasant truth in a distorted fashion.

Our times are much like that moment in the history of Israel when they got right to the border of the Promised Land and sent out spies. After forty days the spies came back with both a majority report and a minority report. The minority report said, "It's a land of milk and honey. Let us go up at once and occupy it. There are giants, but we are well able to overcome them if we recognize that it is the will of God that we go forward, and if we don't lose hope."

The majority report was more pragmatic: "We are not able to go up because the giants are stronger than we." The majority was realistic, which proves once again that majorities may rule but they can't judge with prophetic insight. The prophetic minority always has more to say to a nation than any majority, silent or vocal.

The people, hearing the two reports, wept all night and murmured against Moses and Aaron. "Let's choose a captain and go back to Egypt," they cried. It is always fear that does us in. While love seeks the truth, fear counsels safety. Fear distorts the truth, not by exaggerating the problems, but by underestimating our ability to deal with them.

I don't believe there's a "promised land" for anybody today, but there is a promised time for everybody. I think we can see ourselves, all three billion inhabitants of this planet, right on the border of that time which was predicted in Scripture for those who don't lose their "passion for the possible."

> It shall come to pass in the latter days
>   that the mountain of the house of the Lord

shall be established as the highest of the mountains, . . .
and all the nations shall flow to it . . .
and they shall beat their swords into plowshares; . . .
nation shall not lift up sword against nation,
  neither shall they learn war any more.

—Isaiah 2:2, 4.

We actually could now build a world without borders, a world without famine, a world of unity, a world of peace. But instead of pressing forward, God's children are holding back. Instead of seizing the time, we're losing our grip.

I'm deeply pessimistic, but I'm also hopeful. Hope is the opposite of cynicism. It makes possible preconditions for a better life without any guarantee of their coming about. So while I'm pessimistic, I think we should be deeply hopeful. The worse the situation gets, the more we should try to deal with the problems.

The symbol for today is Good Friday. This is a Good Friday world. Goodness incarnate is stretched out on the cross bequeathing its spirit to the oncoming night. There are giants in the land. There are insuperable obstacles, but as John Gardner once said, "What are giant obstacles if not brilliant opportunities disguised?"

To Christians, resurrection is as politically viable as crucifixion. We should not lose heart. We stand on the border of the promised time and we should move ahead.

My favorite definition of patriotism is that of the ancient Roman, Tacitus. Patriotism, he said, is entering into praiseworthy competition with one's forefathers. I suggest that we should enter into praiseworthy competition with our revolutionary forebears. They declared their independence. Why don't we declare our interdependence?

Why don't we see that the only possible future is a global future? Why don't we acknowledge that the survival unit in our time is not an individual nation but the entire human race, plus its environment?

This should be obvious to us Christians. We've always believed, haven't we, that we all belong to each other, that God made us that way, and that Christ died to keep it that way? Our sin is that we're constantly trying to put asunder what God has joined together. Human unity is not something we're called on to create; it's simply a fact we're called on to recognize and make manifest.

There's an Episcopal collect that speaks of the "God who cares for all as if they were but one and who cares for each as if He had naught else to care for." Every human life, from the point of view of divine dispensation, is not only unprecedented and unrepeatable but also irreplaceable. If Christ did not disdain to die for anybody, who are we to disdain to live for everybody?

But many people are talking of interdependence today. Presidents of multinational corporations will tell us they are no more interested in national borders than the equator, and they mean it. But they're not concerned for social justice, only stability that will serve their own purposes.

Justice is the moral imperative of our time. The third-world problems, at home and abroad, are the moral problems to be solved. Unless social justice comes about, there are going to be no civil liberties. This is true of our country as it is already true of many, many other countries that have failed to solve the problems of social justice. You cannot have freedom without equality. To quote a Puritan forebear, John Winthrop: "We must abridge ourselves of our superfluities for the supply of others' necessities."

Let me make a third point: *If austerity is called for, well and good, for the judgment of the rich not only spells mercy for the poor; the judgment of the rich spells mercy for the rich.*

The United States, with less than 6 percent of the world's population, consumes some 35 percent of the earth's resources. It could be argued that that is simply the price the rest of the world must pay for American happiness. But who will argue that we are a profoundly happy people?

Affluence doesn't buy happiness, though that, fundamentally, has been the American dream. For how many of us has the American dream turned into a nightmare? We cannot live as if life is not consequential. History swings on an ethical hinge. Loosen the hinge and not only history, but nature as well, will feel the shock. Do not be deceived; God is not mocked. The truth is not up for grabs.

If the wealth of rich Americans has to be redistributed, as I certainly believe it does; if the wealth and power of America has to be redistributed abroad; in other words, if austerity is called for, we should rejoice. Austerity is good news. It is a necessary ingredient for human solidarity, the kind of solidarity we see so little of at present, either at home or abroad. There are two ways to be rich: one is to have a lot of money; the other is to have few needs. The second option is very un-American, but profoundly Christian. When there is less wealth, there will be more solidarity.

Now, with that kind of feeling, let me list a few specific things we could be dealing with. One is the food issue. Hunger is the entree into the world community. We should be sending food to the 400 million permanently hungry. Instead of shipping our wheat to Russians so that they can fatten their cattle to satisfy their growing appetite for steaks, we could use it to connect with the suffering of the world.

If we believe all human beings are sacred and have "the right to life," then food too is a right, and the sharing of it is not an option of charity but an obligation of justice.

If food is a right and we believe the world is one, then territorial discrimination in the world is as evil as racial discrimination. Obviously, a world food reserve is called for and it ought to be under some global agency.

A third concern is long-term development for the bottom 30 percent of peoples on the economic ladder. To concentrate on the bottom and make sure we devise policies that really help the poor recognizes that justice is the moral imperative of our time. Many Americans would rather substitute charity for justice. This is evident from the fact that they love to give to charity but hate to pay their taxes. Charity confirms one's sense of power, but taxes reveal our weakness. They say, "It's not yours to begin with, buddy" and keep us from feeling superior.

But the Bible is explicit about this. Charity is the other side of justice, but it is no substitute for justice. If Americans were dedicated to justice, we couldn't "do good," and then, perhaps, we'd begin to get somewhere in the world.

A fourth suggestion is that every nation contribute one tenth of its military budget to meet world needs. Another is to work for a "law of the sea." What a fantastic thing it would be to declare the sea, which is three-fifths of the surface of the globe, a planetary resource to be maintained by a global agency! And of course, we must work for an end of the arms race. The proliferation of nuclear weapons is so insane it's difficult to believe.

A just and global future is our only survival. We can already dimly view its contours. The spies are back. There is a majority report: "We've seen the future and it won't work." And there's a minority report: "We've seen the future and it's ours."

Let's declare a moratorium on "back to Egypt" talk. God is ahead of us as much as he is above us and within us. We probably won't succeed, but nothing else is worth striving for. We cannot act as if failure is morally justified; we must try in our feeble way to do the will of God. There's only an outside chance, but you know, we might make it! We might have a world without wars, without famine, a world at one, a world at peace. There's no technical problem standing in the way; there are only moral and political problems.

No nation can validate its own existence without reference to transcendent reality. For example, our Declaration of Independence reads, "We hold these truths to be self-evident, that all men are created equal." We Americans say, "All." Now, do we mean that—"that they are endowed by their Creator with certain unalienable rights, that among these are

Life, Liberty, and the pursuit of Happiness"? Do we still believe in that, and for all people, because they are endowed by their Creator? If so, we can take these documents and use them as a stimulus to a new spiritual awakening.

Now I don't know where the creditable alternatives are going to originate. There's not much point in expecting them to come from Congress, not Congress alone, certainly. That's not basically its business. Congressmen are supposed to represent their constituents.

The failure is not one of leadership. We should be creating the kind of climate in this country that gives congressmen like John Anderson far more maneuverability because there are constituencies for issues like disarmament, the law of the sea, and the food and hunger problem.

One thing that does seem possible is that congressmen could tell us what bills are coming up and ask us to help build constituencies for them who in turn could demand that the congressman do something about them.

Beyond that, there is something all of us can do. To begin with, everybody can do something on a personal basis about the hunger issue. First of all, we can be informed about the 400 million people who are at the brink of death. *Bread for the World* by Arthur Simon (Eerdmans, 1975) is the best little primer I know on the subject. But there are Lester Brown's and Erik Eckholm's *By Bread Alone* (Praeger, 1974), Larry Minear's *New Hope for the Hungry?* (Friendship Press, 1975), and others. Second, we can fast once a week, or give up one meal, just to stay in touch with suffering. If we ever lose our capacity to connect with suffering, we've had it. Third, we can get our churches or communities to give up one meal a week. Fourth, we can give the money that represents to some agency that will pass it on to the hungry. That's one small way of making a statement. Fifth, we can get schools and institutions to serve several meatless meals each week. And finally, we can do small acts of mercy, get in touch with welfare agencies in our communities and see how we can help. This kind of local concern will push us to a global concern.

We have to have large vision, but the modesty to take small steps. The trouble with some people is they won't take a step unless it's a giant step. Are they giants?

This is a time for consciousness raising. The iceberg has to be melted from the bottom. But as we involve ourselves and take modest steps of action, it will become clearer to us where we need to go.

EXPERIENTIAL EXERCISES

Exercise 1. List the things you were told as a child about America. Which has changed most in your thinking since then? Which can you still affirm?

Exercise 2. Divide the group in half. From a supply of pictures, news magazines and other graphic materials, have each group prepare a collage (using no words or headlines) to illustrate a statement about America. Assign group #1 the statement: "We are proud of our country." Assign group #2: "God help our country with these needs." Twenty minutes should be given to cutting and pasting, and five minutes to each team to interpret its work to the others. Use whatever time remains to dialogue about the meaning of love for one's country.

Exercise 3. Previous to the group meeting, taperecord five minutes from a network news program. Let the group listen to the tape and complete the following statements: "The most helpful news on the tape was _____." "The most discouraging news on the tape was _____." "If I were President, I would _____."

Exercise 4. Take a present-day national issue and brainstorm ways in which a small group, like yours, could influence the outcome. Write all suggestions on a blackboard or newsprint until the group runs out of ideas. Now evaluate (1) which suggestions would be most effective, and (2) which suggestions best fit the Christian lifestyle.

Exercise 5. Jesus said he had "compassion on the multitude, because they . . . have nothing to eat" (Matt. 15:32, KJV). How can we have compassion on the world's hungry in our day? What is our national responsibility toward world hunger? Draw examples from Jesus' life.

7.
INVOLVEMENT

Getting Involved for Our Faith

WHAT do you do as a result of your faith? What action does it lead you to? One young friend of mine explained his response this way: "To know that I am fully accepted by God," he said, "leads me to really want to make something of my life."

Faith and work are inseparably united. "Faith divorced from deeds is lifeless as a corpse," is the way *The New English Bible* translates James 2:26. That's what the name "Faith at Work" implies—a conscious effort by those who believe in Jesus Christ to put their faith to work in everyday life. As Sam Shoemaker, the Episcopal rector who brought this movement into being, used to say, "Let us have no disembodied truth."

The response of faith leads different ones of us along different paths, both individual and social. For some, the "inward journey" is central; for others what's important is the "outward journey."

Often I find myself caught in a tension between the inward and the outward. It was highlighted for me in the contrast between two conferences I attended on successive weekends some years ago. The first weekend was spent exploring issues in our society with some 120 men and women who met as "Evangelicals for Social Concern." "The Chicago Declaration" had come out of an earlier meeting of this group, and now we were together again to discuss specific action proposals. In keeping with our agenda, we met in a rundown hotel south of the loop in Chicago and for three days talked and prayed together seeking to understand the full implications of Christian discipleship.

I was uncomfortable much of the time. I wondered if the blacks in attendance saw me as bigoted. I wondered what traces of "male chauvinism" the feminists could detect in my speech. And I wondered if those who lived in communes or argued for a drastic reduction in our standard of living considered me overly affluent.

Who can feel comfortable in the midst of such wonderings? And how does a Christian decide the questions they provoke? Who lives simply enough, involved enough? What does Christ call us to? Is it the same for all his people? Or does he call us to different lifestyles, each of them suited to the undertaking he has chosen for us? And where, after all, do the demands of the gospel interlock with the glorious good news that we are accepted freely by God's grace?

The following weekend was spent in a magnificent new church building that houses a large creative fellowship of Baptists in Texas. Again we met for three days—some 200 of us—seeking spiritual renewal. The questions this time were largely introspective. What is my relationship to God? to myself? to those around me? How do I use the Bible? prayer? worship? How can I improve interactions with my spouse? my children? my associates at work? my fellow Christians?

Again I felt uncomfortable. I kept wondering how the participants here would have responded to the Chicago agenda—and how, on the other hand, the Chicago participants would have responded to these highly personal questions.

How do faith and work come together? Can we bring them together into one weekend? Can we bring them together in our lives? Is our faith in Christ valid if it does not lead us into caring concern for the world? Are our social concerns valid if they do not arise from a growing personal faith?

Perhaps there is no answer to these questions that can be codified. Perhaps each of us has to live in a tension, facing questions as they come and responding to them without benefit of predetermined answers but in the context of a number of issues that press on us in a given moment.

I can think of three issues that confront me whenever I raise the question of how I ought to be involved in the world:

1. *What needs in the world around me need to be responded to?* By the world I can mean the whole globe or any smaller part of it I choose to focus my attention on. I was raised on stories of foreign missionaries and I think it was good for me. We've narrowed our sights in recent years and become less mission minded, much to our loss. My favorite book as a boy was *Borden of Yale '09,* the story of a gifted young man from a wealthy family who gave his life to Christ so totally that he sought out the most difficult place in the world for missionary service. His research led him to believe that a ministry to Muslims in northwest China would be more difficult than any other and he gave himself deliberately to the goal of reaching them for Christ. Though he was well-rounded in every way (Phi Beta Kappa, a great athlete, and socially skilled) he gave up all thought of marriage, believing he had no right to ask a woman to endure the rigors he intended for himself. He prepared himself for China but never got there, dying of a disease he contracted in Egypt while studying the Muslim religion.

Perhaps the reason why that book left such a mark on me was that my parents went to China to serve as Christians, and I grew up knowing that their dream for their children was that we would follow suit. So something in me rises to the challenge of visionary, global missions to meet human need, whether material, social or spiritual. I want to have a part in them.

But it is more realistic to think of my more immediate world. And then to think of the worlds close to me that I know little or nothing of. There are people who live in "their own little worlds" which I may have never tried to penetrate. The world of race, for example. What races are represented in my small part of the world? Have I made any attempt to know and understand them? How about religious groups other than my own? And people who are confined to institutions: hospitals, nursing homes, prisons? If I were to explore these other worlds what needs might I discover that I could do something about? Might this be one way to find my place of service?

2. *What talents/gifts have I that could be put to use?* What am I good at? What talent do I have that I have never developed? Have I been afraid to look at it and claim it? What ability would I like to develop? What would it take? Is there a way in which it might serve the greater interest of God's kingdom, or does it seem self-indulgent to consider it?

Is it possible that what I like to do is also what God wants me to do? Might he not have made me with the talents I have because he wants me to develop and use them?

Another way of asking the question is this: If you could do anything you wanted to do, with no restrictions such as money or time, what would you do? What does that have to do with your gifts? Is asking these questions likely to lead you away from what God wants for you or to help you bring together your desires and his desires?

3. *How can I unlock the creativity in me?* I have never thought of myself as particularly creative. Ideas didn't come to me readily. I often clammed up when a suggestion was asked for. And I don't relish trying something in public before I've seen someone else try it. To do "my own thing," believing I have an untapped reservoir of creativity in me, has come slowly.

When I first became acquainted with Faith at Work sixteen years ago, one of the intriguing questions Bruce Larson liked to ask people was, "What is your ministry?" The question often came as a surprise to men and women who were not accustomed to think of themselves as having a ministry. Ministry, after all, was for a special class of people, those who were specially gifted or called.

But time after time, as people wrestled with the question, they began to come up with creative ideas of how they could minister for Christ in their daily vocation. Occasionally a man or woman moved into a new vocation in response to the question.

I have always envied friends of mine, like Bruce and Lyman Coleman and Dennis Benson, for whom new ideas seem to explode like popcorn. I first met Dennis for lunch in Pittsburgh several years ago, and while I ate he talked, in his rapid staccato style, of the creativity he was discovering in men and women all over the country as well as sharing some of his own ideas for communicating the Good News. But it was several years before I saw him in action.

At a Youth Specialties conference in Chicago I chose his workshop on designing youth programs. He divided us into groups of eight, seated us in circles and gave each group a familiar object—a marble, an aspirin bottle, a rubber band—and had us interact with it. Our group got the rubber band. We passed it around, reflected on what it represented to us (flexibility, the power to unite, and so on). Then Dennis asked us to design a program around our item. I remember that we came up with a unique program based on rubber bands of many sizes and strengths, complete with Scripture, group discussion and a take-home follow-up project. It was an exciting, creative moment. I went away asking myself, "Why couldn't I have thought of that?"

What is creativity? Can anyone be creative? I'm beginning to discover that creativity is not as elusive a quality as I once thought. All of us can be creative, at least more creative than we are now.

Creativity is making something new, but the newness often consists only in a new arrangement of familiar elements, or an adaptation of something old to a new situation. In a brilliant new book, *The Courage to Create* (Norton, 1975), Rollo May analyzes the creative process and concludes that it is more sweat and tears than a matter of innate gifts. The creative moment usually comes in a moment of relaxation but not so much as a result of the relaxation as of an intensive process of commitment that precedes it. Long hard hours of seeking for the solution to a problem may seem fruitless and then, in an unguarded moment, a creative solution may suddenly present itself, emerging from below-conscious levels when the controls are off. It may come in a dream or on waking in the morning. Albert Einstein used to remark that most of his ideas came while he was shaving.

Creativity seems to require intensity of commitment, willingness to try things and a willingness to fail. That's why Rollo May speaks of the *courage* to create. Creative people are more willing to risk than are the cautious followers. So, if you would be more creative, ask yourself what's holding you back from risking and venturing.

There's something profoundly theological and biblical in all this. Creativity may well be the primary quality of "the image of God" in human beings. Rollo May says, "Creativity is the most basic manifestation of a man or woman fulfilling his or her being in the world." Dorothy Sayers, the English woman of letters and lay theologian, commented years ago in her book, *The Mind of the Maker* (World, Meridian Books), on the Bible's opening statement about God, "In the beginning God created . . . ," "The characteristic common to God and man is apparently that: the desire and ability to make things." And she quotes the Russian philosopher, Nicholas Berdyaev, to the same effect: "God created man in his own image and likeness, i.e., made him a creator too, calling him to free spontaneous activity and not formal obedience to His power. Free creativeness is the creature's answer to the great call of its Creator."

If this is true, creativity is every person's potential and possibility. We can all be co-creators with God, experiencing those "aha" moments of discovery and insight and leaving the imprint of our own uniqueness on the things we do. I write knowing that this can be so. This past year, in my sixtieth year, I have felt more creative in my own ministry than ever before. I'm beginning to find my own way of doing things, not having simply to reproduce what I have seen others do all my life. I have risked new approaches. Some have failed, and I have learned from my failures. Some have succeeded, bringing the profound satisfaction of knowing that I had added something out of my own learning and growth.

I challenge you to be more creative—to question the way in which you are now doing things, to think carefully about what you want to accomplish and to risk new approaches.

Put this challenge "in the hopper," along with your assessment of what needs to be done in your church, your community, your world, and with the particular talents and gifts which you can match to some of those needs.

It may be helpful to listen to the witness of the people whose stories follow. They have faced the same questions you face, and perhaps their responses will hold a clue for you.

"GOD'S NIGHTCRAWLER"

Jean and Eugene McCormick, of Liberty, Indiana, have found a unique means to worm their way into the hearts of young people. They have equipped a large bus with thirty-four sleeping bunks. Traveling at night (using two drivers), the groups they host can spend their daytime hours hiking, swimming or sightseeing, depending on what destination they choose.

The McCormicks call the bus God's Nightcrawler, after the earthworm that emerges at night. "As the nightcrawler is used by fishermen to make their catch," they explain, "so God's Nightcrawler is used to catch the minds and hearts of those traveling on it." It is the bait on the hook for two ardent Christian witnesses.

The McCormicks are farmers who, twenty years ago, began working with senior highs in their small country church. Over the years thirteen foreign exchange students have lived in their home. One of them, a Brazilian, kept in touch with them when he returned home and, when he married, urged the Mc-Cormicks to come to his wedding, which they did. After the wedding they spent three weeks visiting missionaries in Brazil, Argentina, Peru, Colombia and the Canal Zone. So impressed were they with the dedication of men and women who had gone overseas to serve Christ that they came back to Southern Indiana dissatisfied with their own efforts.

They heard of someone with a bus ministry and urged the conference camping commission in their Methodist church to purchase a bus for their youth program, and were turned down flatly. But the McCormicks wouldn't give up and finally the conference voted $13,000 to buy a new bus. On delivery, Eugene and his father went to work building bunks and welding them into the body. Women of the community sewed mattress covers, while the young people helped in every possible way. Bright carpeting was installed on the bus floor. Altogether 500 hours of volunteer labor went into making the bus a traveling hostelry.

Liberty youth took the first trip on God's Nightcrawler. Since then eighteen hundred people have traveled more than ninety thousand miles to such faraway places as Disney World in Florida, the passion play in Eureka Springs, Arkansas, the Smoky Mountains and Atlantic City's famous boardwalk.

The McCormicks have equipped the bus with an eight-track tape player to provide music for their trips. They prepare meals on a Coleman stove, but Jean often brings along baskets of homemade caramel corn and cookies. Her sour cream coffee cakes are a specialty of the trips.

At the back of the bus is an area large enough for group meetings. Singing and group discussions about the Bible, prayer and Christian living often bring young people to take new steps of personal commitment. A candlelight service usually concludes each trip. The McCormicks estimate that two young people plan to enter the ministry as a result of trips on the Nightcrawler. Many others have committed their lives to Christ or joined a local church.

Jean and Eugene McCormick thought the bus ministry would only take a bit of their time when they undertook it, but it has become virtually a full-time job. Cleaning and maintaining the bus between trips, keeping in touch with each young person after a trip, managing the finances and arrangements for the next trip, and scheduling future trips leave little room for any other work.

Fortunately, two of the McCormicks' three children live nearby and help with the farming, freeing Jean and Eugene to do what they love most—witness to their faith in Jesus Christ by creating a happy, harmonious travel experience.

Many happy memories linger in the McCormicks' minds as they think back over the trips they have taken. One that stands out was the trip to Atlantic City. Their busload of teenagers were eager to swim in the Atlantic but on their first morning were greeted with fog and rain. As Jean prayed, Eugene got on the phone to call local churches, looking for some alternate activity for the young people. His first call met a hearty response. The church opened its doors to the teenagers from Indiana. Not only did it have a gymnasium, but the local church youth group showed up to play their visitors in volleyball and stayed on for an evening of spiritual encounter.

On another trip to the Smoky Mountains Eugene McCormick parked the bus in a campground. A seventy-year-old man watched and listened as they sang and talked around a campfire. Later he stopped by to say that he was so impressed, he had gone to the office and paid their parking fee. "It won't hurt for a Baptist to give to Methodists, will it?" he asked.

God's Nightcrawler is booked ahead for six months by different youth groups. Occasionally it carries a group of adults, and has even been used for family camping. To Jean and Eugene the whole experience proves that Christians can find unique adventures for God if they look for them. "Our lives are full and overflowing," they report. "We're thankful that God has chosen to use us."

TURNING DREAMS INTO DEEDS

Millard Fuller

Millard Fuller, as a young businessman in Montgomery, Alabama, made his first million dollars when he was twenty-eight. Three years later when his wife, Linda, threatened to leave him because of his neglect of her and his family, he committed his life to Jesus Christ. Selling his business interests and giving away most of the proceeds, he and Linda began a new life together. Recently we asked Millard, who was working as a development missionary with the Church of Christ in Zaire, to bring up to date the account of his spiritual odyssey. What follows is his story of what one person can do, responding in faith and obedience to some of the needs of the world.

Since Linda and I decided to change our lives that November night in 1965 on a New York City street, God has continuously led us, step-by-step, in what continues to be a magnificent journey of faith. Recently I said to Linda, "I think I'm as busy now as when I was president of our company in Montgomery."

"You're very busy," she replied, "but there's a difference. You don't seem to be under so much pressure."

There is pressure in my work. There are countless frustrations. But a deep joy and sense of contentment compensate for them—a feeling that *I am doing what I should be doing.*

In the summer of 1966 the United Church Board for World Ministries sent us to Africa as "mission interpreters." It was then that the needs of the Equator Region became known to us.

In 1968 I was led to join Clarence Jordan in Americus,

Georgia, where he had founded the Koinonia community. Together we started Koinonia Partners, enlarging the ministry to the poor.

For the next year and a half we lived on a day-to-day basis with Clarence and the people of Koinonia. We talked about the kingdom, and what God wants us to do in his world. Clarence and I spent hours and days talking in his little shack out in the middle of a corn field. We led discipleship schools at Koinonia and elsewhere; we started a poverty housing program; we modernized and expanded the pecan business and began setting up rural industries to give employment to the people.

Clarence began working himself out of his various responsibilities, giving himself more and more to writing and speaking and preaching. A new board of directors was chosen for Koinonia Partners. Clarence officially resigned all his responsibilities. Then—suddenly—he died.

It was an incredible succession of events. It was as if God was laying to rest the old order at Koinonia, and carefully preparing the way for the new. After his death, we continued the work which had been started, without a slowdown or break. We stayed on at Koinonia another three years.

Then in 1972, I felt that God was pushing us out and on, to the next step. The various ministries of Koinonia were going well and there were many capable and dedicated people to continue them. Linda and I talked and prayed about what we should do. We decided to offer ourselves for some service in an underdeveloped country. We had seen so much in our earlier trip to Africa and we were keenly aware that we live in one world and that God loves it all. But where? We called Dr. Robert Nelson, the Africa Secretary of the Disciples Church, and asked about possibilities for work in Zaire, where we had visited. "I do believe your call is providential," Dr. Nelson replied, "for just yesterday a church leader from Zaire was in my office asking if we could send them someone to help with development. I told him no, but now I can tell you yes if you are willing to go." We felt it was a clear sign of where God wanted us, and soon we were on our way to the next venture of faith.

Here in Zaire one door has opened right after another. We are involved in a prison ministry, which means visiting prisoners in the big central prison here in Mbandaka and participating in their worship service each Sunday. With the help of Koinonia Partners, we have obtained nearly three thousand pairs of eyeglasses to be distributed in this area. Even though the population of Mbandaka is one hundred fifty thousand, there are no eyeglasses for sale.

Another project we've launched is "Rise Up and Walk," a program to get wooden legs for the many people here who have lost a leg (mostly from infections—a terrific problem here in the tropics). Linda is in charge of this. To date, we have fitted fourteen people with new legs, and eighteen more are signed up and waiting.

Our biggest project is the poverty housing program. When we came here, both church and government leaders agreed that housing is the most crucial problem in this capital city. Before independence from the French in 1960, a strict policy controlled the city's population. After independence, thousands of people poured in from outlying regions seeking a better way of life. Population doubled five times over but all building stopped. To this day the only building program is that which we launched in 1973 under the sponsorship of the church.

When I came to Zaire to aid the church in "development," a block and sand project the church was running was about to be abandoned. It consisted of a crane mounted on a metal barge (with which sand was scooped from the floor of the Zaire River), two other barges and a tugboat (to transport the sand), a conveyor belt, two block-making machines, a cement mixer and storage rooms. But the equipment was worn out and needed to be repaired or replaced.

We raised money in the United States to keep the project

going and our housing project is an extension of it. When we approached the government for land on which to build, they gave us a tract in the middle of the city called the Bokotola, which means "man who does not care for others." It turns out that this was the "dividing strip" that separated the Africans from the whites in pre-independence days.

The strip was divided into 114 plots and one year ago we began building our first house. Two thousand families have already applied for permission to buy them.

A Fund for Humanity has been set up to make these homes available to poor families. They are sold at cost, with no interest, to people who could not possibly afford to pay the usual interest rates. Monthly payments go back into the fund to help others to have a house. We hope to continue this program after the initial 114 houses are completed. To do so, we will need contributions from overseas.

We are not able to do these things without help from Christians back home. Money is needed for houses, for wooden legs and for Bibles. We present a new Bible to each family that moves into a house, to each recipient of a new leg, and to prisoners in the jails.

I arrived on the scene one day just after the second family had moved into their house. Their little bit of furniture was piled in the living room, and in the middle of all the disorganization, they, with about a dozen friends, were seated in a circle, each person with an open Bible reading Scripture, singing, and praying—thanking God for their good fortune. Tears came to my eyes as I saw their gratitude. It made all the effort worthwhile.

We read in Hebrews that faith is the substance of things hoped for, the evidence of things not seen. Clarence Jordan, I think, made it clearer in his Cotton Patch paraphrase: "Faith is the turning of dreams into deeds; it is betting your life on unseen realities" (Heb. 12:1).*

---

* Clarence Jordan, *The Cotton Patch Version of Hebrews and the General Epistles* (New York: Association Press, 1973).

If we are sad that people can't read the Bible because they have no eyeglasses, if we are sad that people live in miserable shacks and don't have enough to eat, and we act on that sadness by doing what we can, the kingdom comes. We begin to turn our dreams into deeds. We begin to bet our lives on unseen realities. And a sense of defeated sadness is translated into a sadness with hope on the horizon and sureness of victory in the end.

WHO NEEDS SOAP OPERAS?

Dottie Genn

Several years ago I wrote, in FAITH/AT/WORK magazine, the story of a radical change that came to me in a small group that met at a nearby church. I called the story "Sorry for Myself" because it told of long years of illness, or self-pity and weeping over my loneliness and unhappiness. But I had discovered, with help from the members of the group, that God loves me just as I am and that healing could come by receiving and giving his love. My life took a new direction.

The beauty shop I operate behind our house became a place of ministry. Whereas my patrons had had to listen much of the time to my complaints and problems, now I was able to share with them the answers I was finding to my problems.

I have between seventy and eighty customers, many of whom come to my beauty shop once a week; others every other week. Sometimes there are three women at a time in the shop . . . two under driers while I'm working on a third. Or one woman is waiting while I'm finishing up with another.

Many of them tell me this is the highlight of their week. Most of my customers are with me year after year. I don't take a lot of newcomers, and we've become one big happy family, a kind of never-ending sharing group. Each week they come in the same order . . . Sally, Jean and Nila for instance. They get to know each other. I usually have a good half-hour alone with each of them, but the others can hear what we're talking about. And they relate to each other as well as to me. Nila

---

Dottie Genn lives in Camp Hill, Pennsylvania.

comes with a problem and not only shares it with me, but with Jean and Sally, and we all talk about it.

The way I share my faith is just to tell people when something speaks to me. If I feel overwhelmed and grateful about something God has done for me—or shown me—I can't keep it to myself. And if I'm in need of help, I don't mind saying so. Let me give you an example.

It's just one year since my son Dick died at twenty-nine. I was having one of my "Dick days"—missing him terribly—and I decided to turn in *The Upper Room,* one devotional guide I use, to the reading for the day he died. It was Romans 14:8: "If we live, we live to the Lord, and if we die, we die to the Lord; so then, whether we live or whether we die, we are the Lord's."

That so spoke to me that all that day I was able to share it with others. Instead of concentrating on my loss of Dick, I was able to be grateful that he belongs to the Lord and that the Lord gave him to me for twenty-nine years.

I asked one of my customers the other day how she saw me. "Peg," I said, "you knew the old Dottie, and now you know the new. Do you see any difference?"

She thought for a minute and said, "The thing that amazes me about you is all the little nitty gritty things you take to God and how you talk about them. We're all equipped to take big problems to God, but you seem to take everything."

I think that's the secret. It's the everyday things and how we deal with them that can be our most consistent witness. I try not to preach, but just to share what I'm experiencing and discovering.

Reading helps me a lot—reading the Bible and other books that strengthen my faith. I have a little back room upstairs— my hideaway—where I spend a lot of time. And often I share things I have read, when they seem to be appropriate for that day.

One of my customers didn't go far in school and is not a

reader. I loaned her a book, *God's Psychiatry,* and she read it because I had underlined passages that had special meaning to me. So now I pass other books on to her with my underscoring of key passages.

In my business I am able to follow people consistently through their ups and downs, like Claudia for instance. She's a good deal younger than I am, all her friends are either married or engaged, and in her loneliness she had started visiting bars to try to meet men. Well, you know the kind she was likely to pick up there—men who wanted only a superficial friendship.

I shared my faith with Claudia and kept inviting her to go with me to church. She started going regularly and the first thing I knew she had professed to believe in Christ and had joined. But six months later she announced, "I gave it six months and I still don't have a man, so I'm going back to the bars."

I'm glad to say that other people kept after Claudia and one day she went to a "renewal weekend" and now she's really putting God first.

Two weeks ago I wasn't feeling well. I finished work in my shop and was extremely tired. The phone rang and it was Claudia asking if she could come over and talk. "I'm having a problem," she added.

I thought, *Not right now. I don't feel like it and I don't have any answers.* But I told her yes and went upstairs. My New Testament was lying open in the bathroom. I picked it up and my eye fell on a verse that seemed to tell me I was to give Claudia my time and not begrudge it. Then I prayed that God would let his words come through me. What I said to her that day seemed to fit her need, but even more, her coming helped me. Her problem wasn't a big one, but we spent three hours together and I felt much better when she left. In giving my time I received much more.

Sally often kids me by saying I preach good sermons. She

says she always takes something home to share with Joe besides a nice hairdo.

And another one of my customers says, "Who needs soap operas, when there's another chapter each week in Dottie Genn's life?"

Before my son Dick died—when he was going through a very trying time with a kidney problem and finally a transplant—he used to call me as much as ten times a day. I developed the habit of cradling the phone on my shoulder and talking to him while I continued to work. Of course my customers could hear everything I said to him and they marveled at the way I was able to talk. I scolded him at times for indulging in self-pity. I was very exposed and they could see my whole relationship to my son—and to God.

Marty Trostle, my minister at the Methodist church, talked for several Sundays about how we should use our talents for God. I kept wondering what my talent is; there are so many things I can't do. Then someone said to me, "I think you're great on one-to-one witnessing." So I've claimed that as my talent.

But once in a while I have to just follow the nudge I feel and tell a person what I think she should do. Like Marci who lives with her mother and her husband in the same house and for years has treated her husband like an outsider. She explained to me that she could always get another husband but she couldn't get another mother. I had the courage to quote the Bible: "When you're married, you leave your mother and father and cleave to your husband."

I was afraid she wouldn't come back to my shop. But she came back and she has often said that that's what she needed to hear and that she wanted what I have. Well, I let her know what I have is Jesus Christ—not any great consistency of my own but his meeting me in my need. One day Marci had an operation and she told the doctor, "I'm going to be all right because God has spoken to me."

She started going to church—even to prayer meetings—and began to grow. Then she had what appeared to be a heart attack, and was in intensive care for three days. During that time her mother, who had not spoken to her husband in four years, said, "Let me lean on you; I need you."

Now the three of them are living together happily. My part in it all was to be like a receiving station and I know God's power through me helped in a small way their situation.

People can see Christ's life in us best, I think, in the way we handle adversity. I have a son who was born with a cleft palate. So I've spent a lot of time taking him to doctors and giving him special speech therapy. Today he's a speech clinician. He has great compassion for children with handicaps. The first time I heard him sing in public I was just filled with thanksgiving, because for the first few years I prayed simply that he would be able to talk.

My daughter lives ten miles from me. The other day she called to say that the insurance company wasn't going to pay the maternity bills for their new baby because they hadn't been insured long enough. She was crying because she and her husband couldn't see their way out financially.

That morning I had read Matthew 6:26 about how God cares for the birds and how we are of more worth to him than they, and I mentioned it to her. Well, she read it and called me back to say, "What really spoke to me was verse 31: *Therefore do not be anxious, saying, "What shall we eat?" or "What shall we drink?" or "What shall we wear?"*

This is one way witnessing works. When I find something that I'm excited about, I pass it on. Let me give you one more example of how God works. I've carried a load on my conscience for something I did to hurt somebody twenty-four years ago. I asked God to forgive me and thought no more about it until one day last spring when for the first time in these twenty-four years I saw this woman whom I had hurt at a restaurant.

I was uncomfortable, but I let it pass. But a week later I

walked into the same restaurant and there she was again. I asked the Lord, "Do you want me to do something about this? I don't want to reopen an old wound."

When I bumped into her a third time, I got the message. I knew I had to call her, but still I kept putting it off. I actually made myself sick avoiding my duty. I lay around all one day reading and praying. When a friend called, I said, "I have a problem," and I told her about it.

"Do you think I should call her?" I asked.

"It seems to me you know what you have to do," she replied.

"I think I'll wait for another sign." I was dodging.

"Dottie," she said, "you've already been given three signs."

I didn't do anything about it that day, and the next day I was too ill to work. I cancelled all my appointments and went up to my hideaway. I opened the Bible at random and read Romans 8:28: "In everything God works for good with those who love him." That gave me the courage to call her number.

I dialed and without identifying myself, I said, "I called to ask forgiveness for a sin I committed against you years ago. Do you know who this is?"

She said, "Yes, I do. It's Dottie, and I forgive you. I've been wondering why, after all these years, I keep seeing you."

We talked for a while and she told me how she and her husband have both become Christians. And then she quoted me a verse—the same verse, Romans 8:28, that had led me to finally call her. I shared my amazement with her and when she hung up, she said, "I hope we meet again."

A great load was lifted that day. Now I can go to that restaurant—or anywhere—with no fear of running into her—and my guilty conscience. I can go anywhere. And I can tell people that God is at work in my life. I can share my failures as well as my successes and know that he who is at work in everyone can nudge me to say the right thing at the right time.

EXPERIENTIAL EXERCISES

Exercise 1. List the ten most important activities in your life just now. Place an X beside those which were entered into because of your faith. Place an O beside those where your faith enters into the activity in some meaningful way. Discuss your list with two other persons in the group.

Exercise 2. Using today's newspaper, pinpoint two situations of human need. What is the root problem in each one? Can you imagine any action Jesus would take in response to these concerns? What is one thing that you could do this week in response to one of the needs? What could be done by a small group working over a six-month period?

Exercise 3. Select an issue of concern in our world today. As a group, list as many possible steps toward a solution as you can. Do not evaluate these but list all your ideas. Return to the list and indicate which could be done by individuals and which would take group action. Are there any you now choose to do? How might you begin?

Exercise 4. Are there needs in the world today which have been influenced or met by the actions of individual persons? As you recall an example of one, what was the primary factor in that person's response to the need? As a group, list the kinds of things that bring persons to action.

Exercise 5. How did Jesus involve himself in the issues he faced (taxation, temple sales, racial prejudice, hunger, illness and others)? What did his actions have in common? How were they different? Identify and share with your group guidelines for personal involvement in mission.

8.
AUTHORITY

The Bible as Authority

SOONER or later, in any issue we are discussing, whether it be success, or power, or money, the question arises as to the source of authority for what we believe. For Christians the Bible has primary authority as the source of revelation from God and the account of human response to that revelation. But no matter what your view of the Bible's origin and inspiration, it is only in actual life situations that its authority can be demonstrated. When God meets you through some passage in the Bible, the fact carries its own undeniable authority.

I have been reflecting on my own experience with the Bible. The Bible has always been "the Book of books" to me. I have held it in reverence even when I haven't fully understood it. It was the Bible that introduced me to Jesus Christ and through which my image of him has taken shape.

At those key junctures in my life—when I have sought for direction, when I was plagued with doubt and uncertainty, or was questioning and searching—whatever answer I found almost invariably had a "chapter and verse" attached to it, some key passage of the Bible that served as a tent peg to which I could tie my feeble faith.

I went through a period of great uncertainty, however, that

focused on my view of the Bible. I had been taught that the Bible's authority derived from its "inerrancy"—the belief that the original writings were completely free of error (error of any sort whatever: historical, scientific, chronological). I knew the originals were no longer in existence. What we have instead are hundreds and hundreds of handwritten copies and translations which, though remarkably consistent, do have copying errors in them. It is obvious to me now that if God could prevent the writers of the originals from making any mistakes whatever (and the authority of what they wrote rested on that), he could as easily keep the copiers from making mistakes. Somewhere along the line the argument breaks down. It is an argument from the accuracy of texts which do not exist and, hence, cannot be verified. And it is an argument from a mode of operation which is nowhere less evident than in the long history of the careful copying, preservation and translation of the original texts of the Bible.

But I didn't see all this then. My faith was so dependent on a certain view of the Bible that if you had been able to prove a single error in the text I felt I would have to renounce my faith. Whenever I sensed a problem about some of the passages, I trembled with fear. (And, indeed, I had a friend who had had a nervous breakdown over the issue.)

Then one day I decided to reach my own conclusion on the matter by doing a careful study of what the Bible claimed for itself. I took my concordance and looked up every use of the term *word* in all its variations—word of God, word of the Lord, word of Christ, etc.—to see if they were equated with the Bible.

I shall never forget the excitement I felt when it dawned on me that the two were not quite synonymous. The Bible was the written record of a people's history. The Word was the action of God by which he reveals himself. Its usage by New Testament writers did not always carry the same shade of meaning. In the Book of Acts it seemed to be a synonym for *gospel*. Sometimes it seemed synonymous with *truth*. Only

John used it of Christ. And nowhere that I could find did it have to mean the Bible in the strict sense. In fact, on one occasion, it stood in contrast to the Bible, in Acts 17:11 where it says of the Beroeans that when they received the Word from Paul they examined the scriptures daily to see if they harmonized with what they were hearing.

What I discovered was that the Bible's authority was less mechanical and more dynamic than I had ever realized before. To the standard question of the time, "Is the Bible the Word of God or does it contain the Word of God?" I came to reply, "The Word of God contains the Bible." That God has spoken in history, in words and actions, but supremely in Christ—that was the great inescapable truth. The Bible conveys that message and from that fact derives its authority.

One thing this discovery did for me was to lead me beyond "proof-texting"—basing critical beliefs on the narrow interpretation of one single verse or statement in the Bible—and made me seek to know the broad sweep of biblical teaching on any subject.

In theological seminary one of my professors used to say that there are two kinds of Bible students: lumpers and splitters. He was a splitter, a hair-splitter, who saw all kinds of fine distinctions that weren't there. Matthew's "kingdom of heaven," for instance, in his view had to be a different entity from the "kingdom of God" of the other Gospels, just because a different word was used.

But I have become a lumper, seeking for that which different statements and different personal experiences have in common, just as I seek to discover the unity between my experience and the experience of others so that I can lay down a bridge of understanding to walk across. I am more and more impressed with the commonality of human experience. Under the surface we are all pretty much alike. We want similar things, we react in similar ways and the grace of God comes to us all.

Another learning is that as I have come to know myself better the Bible has opened up more clearly. I now see that many of its truths were closed to me until I came to the place in my own experience and awareness that gave me the capacity for understanding. Just as a child cannot understand the experiences of an adolescent, or an adolescent that of a mature adult, so the life-truth of the Bible unfolds when we are ready for it and capable of living into it.

So it is not enough to study the Bible; we must study human nature as well. The more we know of history, of literature, of the behavioral sciences and the more we live into what we discover in our own experience, the more alive the truth in the Bible can become to us. Some of the narrowest biblical interpreters are those who read nothing but the Bible. And I am convinced that they know the Bible *less* for doing so. The Bible is unique in the saving truth it imparts. But all truth is God's truth and the broader and deeper our understanding, no matter from what source we derive it, the more facility we will bring to our reading of the Bible.

In recent years I have formulated a process for Bible study which I call triangulation. Just as a surveyor, in identifying the altitude and position of a certain point, sets up a transit and gets a reading on two other points, I get my bearings by relating three different points: the Bible, the church and my own experience. By the church I mean whatever understanding of what has been experienced and understood by Christians down through the centuries, as well as my experience with other Christians with whom I share experience and understanding today. It is important to me to be part of a small group of Christians where I can try out my insights and get their feedback. There is a place for solitary Bible study, but there is also a great need for checking out our conclusions with others and submitting ourselves to the kind of correction that can come in the interchange with others. After all, it is the community that produced the Bible and not the other way around. First the fellowship of believers existed. The writing followed.

If I am reading the Bible I need to triangulate my understanding with two other points: my personal experience and the common experience of the body of Christians which I can touch in a small group or through my understanding of church history, or both.

If I am trying to understand some point in my experience I need to check it against the Bible and the fellowship. These three points, then, serve as framework within which I gain some real sense of authority about what I understand and believe. I must always admit the possibility of error. Absoluteness is beyond human reach. But I can know and believe with sufficient authority to make decisions and to commit my life to certain directions. And taking those directions will bring its own sufficient proof of the validity of my choices.

In recent years a new dimension of Bible study has begun to open up to me as I've started to get into it with my *feelings* as well as my *thinking*. This has come about through internal urging as I've gotten more and more in touch with my own feelings.

There have also been external influences. I'll always be indebted to the friend who introduced me to Archie Matson's *A Month with the Master* (Harper and Brothers, 1948), which is unfortunately now out of print. Following a style of meditation that St. Ignatius prescribed for Jesuits in his "Scriptural Exercises," Matson takes thirty-three stories from Luke's Gospel and, after setting the stage with necessary historical and cultural information, guides the reader in how to reconstruct the stories in his imagination. One is encouraged to see the setting, hear the sounds, smell the smells, and identify with the feelings of each person in the story. When practiced successfully, the Bible story literally becomes one's own story and connections are made to contemporary situations.

The story of a paralytic raises questions about our own emotional or spiritual paralysis. The story of a blind beggar suggests areas in which we are blind or dependent. A prostitute's story forces us to ask how we may be prostituting ourselves. And so on.

My most recent gift is a small group of men and women in

the church which I attend who meet each week to read Scriptures and to do more than simply talk about it. Often we act it out in role-play. We find that by moving physically and acting out our understanding of a Bible passage, we engage our feelings and make more connections with "where we are" emotionally and spiritually. With table and chairs we have built a vine and branches and, in the process, surfaced our feelings toward Christ and each other. We have, like Job, "sat among the ashes" voicing our complaints. In response to Paul's description of the Body of Christ, we have recognized our gifts and positioned ourselves in the Body accordingly. We are discovering that there is no end to the possibilities of absorbing the truth through our bodies and our emotions as well as our minds.

But the nature of the Bible's authority is an issue each of us needs to settle for ourselves. Perhaps the articles by J. J. Lamberts and Karl Olsson will help you in your own thinking.

DO WE TAKE THE BIBLE FOR GRANTED?

J. J. Lamberts

We were watching one of those science motion pictures that the people at Moody Bible Institute used to produce—probably still do—with such dazzling skill and artistry. The subject was the human heart. First the film showed the outside of a beating heart, and then it moved inside the heart to let us see one of the several valves.

For a moment I stared at that valve with a kind of disbelief; it looked so casually simple. Three triangular leaves kept folding back and forth to meter out the blood, but the leaves themselves were not neatly symmetrical at all. In fact, the valves you can buy at a hardware store look a lot more precisely machined than the homely old heart valve.

Oddly, the heart valve reminded me of the Bible. You must admit that our church confessions and creeds are a lot tidier and look much more efficient. But they remind me in turn of the valves from the hardware store—polished and plated and to the point, yet bound to wear out after a while and needing to be replaced. The Bible, on the other hand, like that plain old heart valve, keeps sending a stream of warm blood through the body—in this instance, the Body of our Lord.

Now even though that part of the body of Jesus Christ which seeks to respond in obedience under the name of Faith at Work is a highly diverse and far scattered company, there are some pretty important matters which its adherents hold in common. Unlike our many and sundry denominations, Faith at Work is not a confessional body and there are no "admission

J. J. Lamberts is professor of English at Arizona State University, Tempe, Arizona.

standards." Somewhere in the magazine there has always been a brief statement describing Faith at Work fellowship, but that gets reworded and rephrased from time to time. There are indeed things that bring us together in agreement or common interest—things like wholeness or healing or personal relationships or witnessing or the relevance of the church itself. These we hold up to the light now and then so that we can look at them together.

Yet there are other matters which we mention only in passing, if at all, because we so much take them for granted. I suppose it's like telling your wife that you love her, not to allay any possible doubts, but to affirm something that's basic to a relationship.

The authority of the Bible as the Word of God is one such matter in the community of Faith at Work. It may be that we too much take it for granted. Perhaps we should remind ourselves of that as well.

A good deal of ignorant flapdoodle has been said and written about the Supreme Court decision on Bible reading in the schools, with little effect, seemingly, on the reading of the Bible itself. It is a well-attested fact that courses in the Bible as literature, or something closely related, are on the increase in our high schools, colleges, and universities, and these have proved to be enormously popular. After all, the Bible is literature and it has profoundly influenced English writing from the very beginning till now. But in order to study the Bible as literature, the student chiefly needs to know something about the nature of literature itself. It comes as no surprise then that some of the most skilled teachers have been or are self-professed atheists. At least they recognize literature when they see it.

To read the Bible as the Word of God, however, a person needs entirely different credentials. Then it becomes not an intellectual study, but a spiritual one, and we can understand why persons who can barely read at all are among those who discover things which, as the Lord once said, are hidden from "the wise and prudent" but "revealed to babes."

There are those, of course, who read the Bible merely for the sake of curiosity, to discover if possible what believers find so meaningful. And I am sure there are many who read it faithfully from habit or a sense of obligation—just as I did before Jesus Christ touched my life. And some read it for luck, on about the same level as the horoscope in the daily newspaper.

But the believer adds a different dimension. To him the Bible is the authentic and authoritative Word of God. Like the heart valve, it looks casually put together—history and poetry and law and drama and prophecy and biography and correspondence—all of it in one book with little apparent heed to the general organization. One suspects that maybe God wanted it that way; certainly the student of the Bible is the more challenged to follow the injunction, "Search the Scriptures."

We realize that there are different approaches. Unfortunately, the most usual way to engage in Bible study seems to be to do it by proxy, that is, to rely on a clergyperson or Sunday school teacher to undertake the necessary preparation. This is not to suggest that there is anything wrong with Bible-based preaching or Sunday school instruction. Jesus Christ preached a sermon from a text in Isaiah, Peter spoke on a passage from Joel and from several of the Psalms, and Stephen gave a detailed exegesis of the history of Israel, based almost entirely on the five books of Moses. But unless Bible preaching is supplemented and reinforced by regular personal Bible study, we produce "spiritual vampires," persons, that is, who are always taking in, never satisfied, and never capable of becoming productive for the service of the kingdom.

As teaching methods go, the lecture method—which is what most sermons really are—ranks fairly low in effectiveness. Paul was far more effective with his letters than with his preaching. These letters were read to and discussed by the various local congregations—the equivalent of our "small groups"—for most of the first three or four centuries of Christianity. We tend to forget that the early "churches" were no more than scattered groups of Christians who could come together in a home—not a church building as we think of it.

Group Bible study has been one of the means by which many members of the Faith at Work fellowship have come together and remained together. It is common knowledge among those who have had experience in such matters that small groups which form simply for the sake of coming together, or in order to discuss a book—any book—presently run out of things to discuss, and they disband. But a group committed to a faithful study of the Bible as the Word of God may well go on for years and years.

What this means is that God seeks to speak to us through his word as a community. Actually being this community—half a dozen couples, for instance—is seldom as easy as it looks. Apart from the demands of fundamental honesty and mutual trust which the nature of such a group presently generates, there is the down-to-earth matter of protocol. Some members of the group will be inclined to defer to a clergyperson or to someone who has had even a smattering of theological training. And on the other hand, it is also possible to depend altogether on what this or that commentary says, rather than let the Bible speak for itself. Before long the members of the group must come to realize that each person has unique and valuable gifts in reading and interpreting what God's word has to say. Otherwise, it is not a group but an audience.

And this means further that each of us has an obligation to be his own Bible scholar, which is to say that there is room for private enterprise in Bible study. While Jesus Christ spoke to enormous crowds of people, he made some of his most profound revelations to a single person at a time—to Nicodemus, for example, or the Samaritan woman at Jacob's Well.

Each of us must, of course, have our own personal method. The most familiar one is to underline passages with a pencil. Another is to make notations in the margin. But very few Bibles have wide enough margins for much significant comment.

I am sure all of us have studied the Bible with the help of a commentary, but how many have considered writing their own? To dedicate part of one's "quiet time" for several years to writing a personal and private commentary on a particular book of the Bible is a challenging discipline. The method is really very simple. You provide yourself with a looseleaf notebook and a pen or pencil. Then copy a verse or part of a verse from the Bible. (I happen to prefer the Revised Standard Version since it is in reasonably modern English.) The next thing is to study that verse until you see something there that you've never seen before. Don't be in a hurry; don't reach for a commentary. Trust the Holy Spirit to open your eyes.

It does not really matter how cleverly we read the Bible. Nor does it matter how deeply we search for hidden meanings. The important matter is *what* we find. There is something for each believer. And it is specifically for that person.

Many of the world's great religions have their sacred books, and many of the cults that lay sort of a backhanded claim to being Christian display a book of writings by their founder which presumes to explain or supplement or supercede or "correctly translate" the Bible. A curious mark all of them share is a special kind of sameness among those each one seeks as its adherents, or likewise it presently enforces a kind of sameness upon them. Christianity, quite the contrary, is unique in that we are able time and again to affirm each other as members of a community with a bond in Jesus Christ that makes us one, yet at the same time we are able to affirm one another as individuals with distinctive gifts and often highly diverse personalities.

A Creator who makes every snowflake different from every other one will scarcely employ a single mold when he performs an even greater miracle—making a new saint out of an old sinner. Each of us is, in fact, a "custom product" from the hands of our Maker. And the Bible, as Ralph Osborne once remarked, is the "Manufacturer's Handbook."

IS THE BIBLE TRUE?

Karl Olsson

Our copy of *Time* was delivered on Christmas Eve just as we were about to begin our ethnically oriented Yuletide celebration: the food, the drink, the Gospel, the carols, and the gifts. On the cover of that "good news" magazine was an elaborate drawing of the wise men with the question: "Is the Bible True?"

The immediate effect of this angelic tiding on the assembly was resentment. Who had invited Rudolph Bultmann and the Missouri Synod to our joyous mysteries?

In retrospect, however, the raspy bluntness of the question was not without its good effect. I began to ask again why and how I believe the Bible to be true.

When we ask if something is true, we usually mean if the thing talked about squares with reality. Did the thing reported actually take place? We check out the validity of the report by testimony or by inferences from circumstances.

Put into that context the question, "Is the Bible true?" could mean, "Can we believe that *all* the things reported in the Scriptures—speeches, miracles, genealogies—check out?" Are they true in the sense that we believe the multiplication table to be true as the testimony of an honest and capable person in a court trial?

There is another view which claims a thing true not because it actually happened but because it is the kind of thing that could have happened. Assuming God to be powerful, wise, and loving, he could have acted as the Bible reports him to have acted, but he may not, in fact, have done so. This shifts the place of truth from the record of happenings to the char-

157

acter of God and puts my trust in him rather than in what he is reported to have done.

I believe that both views are understandable. An enormous amount of energy has been expended to prove the Bible reliable or unreliable in the first sense. Those who have argued for the literal truth of the Scriptures down to the last detail have done so to credential the Author and to make his story about himself as well as his promises reliable.

Those who have taken the opposite tack have insisted that we are interested, not in a perfect book, but in a living God and that the literalists make the Bible, not God, great. What is important is not the historical happening but how our faith interprets events and makes them meaningful in our life and the life of the church. This stance has freed the nonliteralists to make myth and legend of as much of the Bible as seemed reasonable. The hard question: did this actually happen? has not been relevant to their faith.

I am a middle person in this sort of discussion. I do not believe that the Bible has to be inerrant in detail to be God's Word, and I believe that the Bible contains much in story, parable, and poetry which points to the greatness of God without being historically factual. But I believe that the biblical revelation—the combination of God's Word in history—is true. I believe that in that unity of event and truth the major acts of the drama actually happened.

I believe in God's creation of the world and of people, the mysterious emergence of sin, the choice of Abraham and his descendents to be the carriers of the burden and the blessing of salvation; I believe in the exodus and the deliverance and God's dialogue with his people through prophets, priests, and kings. I believe in the Incarnation of the Word—the life, teaching, wonders, passion, death, resurrection, and exaltation of Jesus. The coming of the Spirit, the acts of the apostles, the birth of the church pointing to the Parousia, and the last things also have this flesh and blood credibility for me. It will not to make them multidimensional myths or the brain children of an eschatological faith community.

So much for the happening. But the happening without the Word is only half the truth. I do not believe that the interpretation of the happening any more than the happening is left to human imagination. I believe that the Bible was written by very human people but that the ultimate author is the Holy Spirit. It is he who makes the truth of the happenings available to us. Because of him, prophecy can wait patiently for fulfillment and fulfillment can be given clarity by prophecy. When Jesus was vested with the robe of the Suffering Servant, it was the Spirit who made the connection with Isaiah 53. The Spirit is the source of our "aha" in the presence of the Lord.

Thus far we have talked about two levels of truth: the truth *of* the happening and the truth *in* the happening. But there is a third. There is the truth *of* the happening and *in* the happening becoming an active truth for me. Better yet: my entering into the truth and experiencing it as personal and relational.

The Gospel of John tells us that when Jesus appeared before Pilate, our Lord said, "For this was I born, and for this I have come into the world, to bear witness to the truth. Every one who is *of the truth* hears my voice" (John 18:37).

What is it to be *of the truth?* I believe that it is opening myself to the Holy Spirit, being "born from above" (John) or a "new creature in Christ" (Paul) or a member of the Body of Christ. From this new stance I see biblical truth (happening and interpretation) not just as propositions I must defend or analyze critically but as God's living Word to me in the midst of my humanity and my relationships.

Until the Bible becomes God's Word in that personal, relational way, it is like grain which is not allowed to germinate. A Christian mystic once said, "What does it matter that Christ was born in Bethlehem if he is not born again in my heart?" I happen to believe that it is terribly important that Christ was born in Bethlehem, but I agree with the mystic that it is, at best, only half the truth.

This personalized truth despite its importance, has been set aside in much of the history of the church. We have, to continue the figure of the grain, spent untold amounts of energy sacking, transporting, and distributing it (or subjecting it to scientific analysis). Every Sunday morning in thousands of Sunday schools and church services we have emptied sacks of it on people, but not much of it has been allowed to fall into good ground and to bear fruit.

In a recent workshop on Bible study, I swept around a circle of adults—some twenty of them—and asked them to give me one vivid symbol or impression of the Bible from their first twelve years. The results were not very encouraging. Some remembered a few rousing good stories; others recalled an angry God; still others thought of a black book. Very few remembered the Bible as a book to which they might voluntarily turn for comfort or even guidance. Even those from conservative homes considered the reading of the Bible as a pious chore laid on them by their parents.

I am afraid that what was true in the childhood of these people is generally the case for many Christians today. The Bible is not true in the sense that it is a *living* truth. Too often, despite my excitement about relational Bible study, I do not let the Bible be alive for me. And yet when I bestir myself and take time to read and to listen, I am seldom disappointed. I may hear things I don't want to heed, but even in the tough notes I hear the Word spoken which is my refuge and solace, my judgment and my salvation.

EXPERIENTIAL EXERCISES

Exercise 1. Select a Bible passage that has interest to the group and is no longer than twelve or fourteen verses. Let each person in the group silently read the passage over and over again from his/ her own Bible, for about ten minutes. Make notes if you wish. Then have everyone in the group reflect on the passage and develop a restatement of its message in their own words. Ask yourself the questions: What is the main idea? What was the feeling of the author when this was written? Is there some conviction or guideline hidden in this passage?

Second, allow the group to discuss and reflect on: What is the meaning of this passage as we see it from our perspective two thousand years later? Can we identify some feelings, needs, or human situations that are still common?

Third, let the group reflect on the passage individually, asking the question: What does my understanding of this Scripture demand in my relationship to God or other persons? What would I do if I were to take this passage seriously in my own life? In groups of three, discuss the outcome of this last time of reflection and discover ways in which you can help clarify or reinforce decisions that persons make in light of the passage.

Exercise 2. Relational Bible study is a way of coming to grips with the internal meanings of a passage. The process is as follows: Select a passage from one of the Gospels that is either a narrative or a parable.

1. Try to read the story so that you can visualize what is happening. Try to be there and to experience the setting in your own mind and imagination.
2. Find the element in the story with which you can identify. This will probably be a character or a situation. Imagine your-

self being that person and decide what about that person in the situation makes you feel more a part of him/her.

3. What is the Good News for the person in the story, and for you? What about the situation mediates the love of God in Jesus Christ in a way that you can understand and claim it for yourself?

4. Name the story. Give the story a designation that will help you remember the gospel message for you in it. Since this name will mainly recall the truth for yourself, it may be either humorous, have a private meaning, or may come out of the story itself.

After everyone has had a chance to go through this process with the passage they have chosen, in groups of three take about twenty minutes to share with each other your relational Bible study. Try to help each other understand the ramifications of the insights of the studies.

Exercise 3.   Divide a sheet of notebook paper vertically by drawing a line down the middle. On one side of the line write in your own words a "translation" of a favorite passage of Scripture. Try at every point to use your words in place of the words that you find in the Bible you are using. The object of this portion of the exercise is not to develop a scholastically sound translation as much as it is to get in touch with the meaning of the passage in a way that you can clearly understand it. On the right side of the page, begin to write your reflections, your "commentary" on this passage. In trying to understand the meaning of the passage, use, as much as possible, experiences out of your own life, feelings that you yourself have had, or insights that have come to you out of your own spiritual journey. This is an exercise in trying to explain the Scriptures out of a life context which is your own. Share together the results of your time of reflection and translation in groups of three.

Exercise 4.   (To follow any one of the above.) In the light of looking at a passage out of our own experience and understanding, what do you understand to be the meaning of the authority of the Scriptures? Do you see ways in which your interpretations or understandings of the Scriptures might be valid for other persons? Do you see ways in which they would not be valid or helpful to other persons? Is the Scripture a "living Word of God" which carries on a dialogue with believers as they read?